FETTERS OF INJUSTICE

Consultation on Ecumenical Assistance to Development Projects, Montreux, Switzerland, 1970

FETTERS OF INJUSTICE

Report of an ecumenical consultation

on

Ecumenical Assistance to Development Projects

26 — 31 January, 1970, Montreux, Switzerland

edited by

Pamela H. Gruber

WORLD COUNCIL OF CHURCHES

GENEVA

1970

German Version: Ungerechte Fesseln öffnen

© Copyright 1970 World Council of Churches, Geneva

Printed in Germany by Otto Lembeck, Frankfurt am Main and Butzbach

Cover: John Taylor

Table of Contents

Editor's note:

The use of the term "developed" and "developing" countries was questioned repeatedly at the consultation. The concept of development as elaborated in the report of Group I is quite different from the assumptions behind the current use of the terms "developed" and "developing" countries. However, for want of better terms, this report continues to use "developed" and "developing" to distinguish between those countries with a high Gross National Product and those with a low Gross National Product.

Introduction

World cooperation for development has become a major concern of the churches and the ecumenical movement. Numerous confessional and ecumenical gatherings held on national, regional and world levels during the past few years clearly demonstrate this fact. In many countries, churches are taking new initiatives to promote better living conditions for all people.

Perhaps the most significant ecumenical expression of this concern to promote development came from the Fourth Assembly of the World Council of Churches at Uppsala, Sweden, in July, 1968. Development was a major theme, permeating the entire Assembly. One of the six sections, "World Economic and Social Development", urged Christians everywhere "to participate in the struggle of millions of people for greater social justice and for world development". This theme was also mooted in Section IV, "Towards Justice and Peace in International Affairs". In its message, the Assembly declared, "We heard the cry of those who long for peace; of the hungry and exploited who demand bread and justice; of the victims of discrimination who claim human dignity; and of the increasing millions who seek for the meaning of life". It asserted that "the ever widening gap between the rich and the poor, fostered by armament expenditure, is the crucial point of decision today".

It is recognized that the most important contribution that the Christian Churches can make in this matter is in the promotion of education for development, in changing the attitudes of people, in mobilizing public opinion towards fundamental changes in the social, economic and political structures on national and international levels. The World Council of Churches is encouraging and assisting the churches in this direction through its various units and through the Committee on Society, Development and Peace (SODEPAX) jointly established with the Pontifical Commission Justice and Peace of the Roman Catholic Church.

The churches are also involved in an expanding programme of assistance to development projects. Various mission and service agencies of the churches, which have a long record of assistance to development projects, are increasing their efforts. The Uppsala Assembly encouraged the churches to advance further in this direction and appealed to them to give sacrificially above and beyond the amounts spent on mission and other programmes and to "explore how international foundations could be set up through which endowments and other church funds may be responsibly invested for development".

Since the Uppsala Assembly, a number of churches have taken various types of initiative to make available increasing amounts of funds for development purposes and asked the help of the World Council of Churches in the proper utilization of such funds. The churches in the less materially developed countries also expressed their concern about the proper chanelling of resources, finance and personnel, from outside. At the same time, questions were raised by development experts on the rationale and patterns of the churches' involvement in development programmes and projects.

In view of this situation, the Central Committee of the World Council of Churches called for a world consultation to discuss the use of church funds in development projects and to advise the Council and its member churches. It also appointed a Planning Committee for the consultation, composed of the following people, representative of four major units of the World Council of Churches: Dr. Tracey K. Jones, Jr. (Chairman, Division of World Mission and Evangelism), Mr. Albert Laham (Chairman, Division of Ecumenical Action), Prof. S. L. Parmar (Chairman, Department on Church and Society) and Dr. D. H. Thimme (Chairman, Division of Inter-Church Aid, Refugee and World Service). Subsequently, the Planning Committee, in cooperation with a Staff Working Party on Development appointed by the General Secretary of the World Council of Churches, prepared and organized a consultation on "Ecumenical Assistance for Development Projects" held in Montreux, Switzerland, from the 26th-31st January, 1970. This volume is the official report of this consultation.

A long and steady process of preparation preceded the Montreux Consultation. During the spring and summer of 1969, a document prepared by staff on this subject was widely discussed at national and international levels, especially at certain meetings of the World Council of Churches. In the light of such discussions and in view of the proposed programme of the consultation, five papers were prepared by four members of the World Council of Churches staff and a member of the SODEPAX staff. These and a paper entitled "Issues for Preparatory

Discussion" were studied and examined by a large number of individuals, groups and certain official bodies of a few churches in the various parts of the world. Many comments were received at the headquarters of the World Council of Churches. Incorporating the most relevant insights from such comments, the staff prepared five 'position papers', which were used as the basic documents for the five working groups at the consultation.

The Montreux Consultation was fortunate in securing the participation of a good selection of people. There were altogether 88 participants, excluding the large number of staff involved in the organization. They came from some 40 countries, representing various confessions and church traditions. There were also three representatives from the Roman Catholic Church. Participants were also a good mixture of development experts, professional workers, representatives of the United Nations and its related agencies, church executives and theologians. Geographically speaking, more than half of the participants came from Asia, Africa and Latin America. Four representatives came from Eastern Europe and the rest from Europe and North America. If the consultation lacked balance it was in the proportion of women and youth.

Perhaps one of the striking features of the Montreux Consultation was the decisive rôle of the representatives from the so-called "Third World". Dr. Charles D. Sherman, Financial Consultant to the President of Liberia and formerly Secretary of the Treasury of Liberia, was the Chairman. Among the six speakers, three came from the continents of Asia, Africa and Latin America. There was also equal representation from the Third World in the leadership of the five working groups.

The major part of this report consists of the reports of the five working groups as adopted by the entire consultation, the six major addresses given at the consultation and the opening addresses by the Chairman, Dr. Charles D. Sherman, and the General Secretary of the World Council of Churches, Dr. Eugene Carson Blake. For those readers who are interested in a summary of the major debates, issues and insights from Montreux, an article by Dr. Reinhild Traitler is included.

It is sometimes said that ecumenical consultations are seldom followed through and acted upon. It is hoped that the Montreux Consultation will not receive such negative comments. There are sufficient indications to believe that the churches are taking seriously the findings of Montreux. The World Council of Churches, for its part, has already taken certain steps to follow up Montreux. The Executive Committee of the World Council of Churches at its meeting in Geneva in February, 1970, received with enthusiasm the reports of Montreux and decided to establish a Commission on the Churches' Participation in Development as recommended by the consultation. This proposal as adopted by the Executive Committee is also published in this volume, together with a letter from the General Secretary to the member churches, mission and service agencies.

The staff of the World Council of Churches and the Planning Committee of the Montreux Consultation are indeed extremely grateful to the Chairman of the consultation, the six speakers, and the chairmen and secretaries of the five working groups for their able leadership. They are also grateful to all the participants, especially the representatives from the United Nations, its related agencies and the World Bank.

Judging from the numerous comments and reports received from participants and others, and those which appeared in the press and on radio and television in various languages and countries, one can speak of the Montreux Consultation as a significant event in the history of the ecumenical movement. In how far it was a decisive event can only be determined on the basis of the response of the churches in various parts of the world and the initiatives which they take in the coming months and years.

C. I. Itty

PART I:
Adresses

Opening Remarks

by Charles Sherman

My dear friends,

May I first of all welcome you to this Consultation on Development, the results of which I sincerely hope will bear abundant fruit, to the glory of God and the edification of His children wherever dispersed over the face of the earth.

There is a Spanish expression that a fool often does in the end what a wise man does in the beginning. Therefore, we dare not risk entering upon so momentous an undertaking without invoking God's presence and guidance from the beginning, and throughout our deliberations.

Let us pray:

O almighty and eternal God, creator of the universe,
Thou who alone can'st encompass and make anew all things,
renew within our hearts the knowledge of Thy truth that
our eyes may recognize that all things come of Thee and we
can, as stewards, only offer Thee of Thine own.
In all that we shall seek to do we implore Thy blessing.
May Thine abiding presence direct our minds, rule our wills
and govern our hearts — so that all our work, begun, continued
and ended in Thee may be of enduring value to Thy kingdom and
service to humanity, forever. Amen.

And now, I would like to invite you to reflect on two sections of the Holy Gospel as recorded by St. Luke. The first covers verses 13, 14 and 15 of the 12th chapter and reads as follows:

"And one of the company saith unto Him, Master, speak to my brother that he divide the inheritance with me."

"And He said unto him, Man, who made me a judge or divider over you?"

"And He said unto them, take heed, and beware of covetousness: for a man's life consisteth not in the abundance of the things which he possesseth."

The second passage is taken from the 6th chapter, verses 32 to 35:
"For if ye love them which love you, what thank have ye, for sinners also love those that love them.

"And if ye do good to them which do good to you, what thank have ye, for sinners so do even the same.

"And if ye do good to them which do good to you, what thank have have ye? Sinners also lend to sinners to receive so much again.

"But love ye your enemies, and do good, and lend, hoping for nothing: and your reward shall be great, and ye shall be the children of the Highest: for He is kind unto the unthankful and to the evil".

The excellent conference documents which have been sent out in advance of our arrival are, in my opinion, scholarly and clear. The options available have been thoughtfully and carefully exposed, the alternatives discretely delineated and developed. In the next few days, we shall be further instructed and enlightened by the erudite addresses of our distinguished guest speakers who will draw from their rich backgrounds and practical experience.

I am, therefore, certain that the profound insights and conclusions we shall reach together can be translated into worthwhile and utilitarian recommendations, lending themselves to rewarding action and rational implementation.

I cannot avoid saying how pleased I was to notice in all the Conference definitions the recurrent theme that development should not be limited in scope or conception to material possessions. There are other indispensable components.

Faced as we are with the pervasiveness of poverty and disease; surrounded by the blight of ignorance and the scourge of illiteracy; confronted by the intransigence of those who control the apparatus of power and the mechanism of wealth, who are unwilling to share these on any basis other than the self-defeating power of brute force; staring into the yawning chasm which separates the teeming millions of disinherited from the citadels of established social privilege and bastions of entrenched inequality of opportunity, we cannot but realize the unwisdom of dwelling for long in the shadows of remedial acts of merciful pity or pompous charity.

14

Our problems need more fundamental and drastic efforts. Neither can the leaders of the Third World be considered totally blameless in many instances where priorities are established of questionable viability. We need surgery that will eventually eliminate the very roots of evil and create the basis for a workable blue-print for progressive amelioration of the ravages of poverty and disease. The need for a different way of handling these evils is intuitively sensed by today's youth the world over. They rightly reject the excuses given for the existence of these conditions. Neither will they accept uncritically the norms by which we measure individual success in the community, or the efforts of contemporary society to overcome their problems.

Much is being done to feed the hungry and to meet emergencies. Perhaps not in sufficient degree, but it is being done. I venture to suggest that it is not enough that the Church should become only one more avenue or source of material aid. Our aim must be broader and more comprehensive. Our techniques should be bold and not fast bound to staid traditions, no matter how efficient they may have been in older or other contexts. Above all, our motivation must be transcendental.

It is not easy to insulate one's self from the light of contemporary intellectual evidence or to cast off the deadweight of cultural intrusions. In this connection, with your permission, I will recall my own experience in connection with the organisation of the African Development Bank at Khartoum. A few delegations suggested that each member country should have an equal vote despite the amount of money it contributed to the capital; and that priority in lending should be given to the countries with poorer infrastructures. My reaction was instantaneous and unequivocal: no serious minded banker could accept such sentimental talk.

Several years have now passed and as I have watched the rather slow progress of poor countries in Africa in comparison with the rich, I have come to suspect that something is fundamentally wrong with such familiar, trustworthy power mills which persistently grind out predictable results that they more often than not provide development without accelerating growth.

What shall we say to the vast majority of the citizens of the affluent societies who are indifferent or case-hardened to the world of need next door. What shall we say to the liberals who are only concerned with moral contentions on behalf of the revolutionaries and radicals?

What shall we say to the American Negro youth who, upon being invited to help with the struggle for African redemption ten years ago, replied, "Man, I have not lost anything in Africa, what am I going to find?"

What shall we say to the Mormon Elders who claim that it is the will of God that coloured people should forever be numbered as hewers of wood or drawers of water; what shall we tell those Dutch Reformed who consider coloured races beneficiaries of the curse on Noah's sons?

What do I say to the character from the Third World who exclaims that our people will be emancipated when they stop stealing chickens and learn to successfully rob banks?

Whatever we may say to the indifferent, the sophisticated or the hostile, if the answer is based on science, it may change with new discoveries and the invention of new techniques. Whatever the cultural answer, it may be prejudiced and disoriented. A single moral answer is not enough. The only complete reply is a Christian answer whose logic and rationale are rooted in the teachings and example of Christ. In this age of supreme doubt, Christians must be the salty salt of the earth or they shall be cast down and trodden under the feet of countless men, including those who do not know why or where they are going and care less.

In the 17th chapter of the Acts of the Apostle, Paul and Silas and some of the other early Christians upon reaching Thessalonica were described in a dispatch in these terms: "These that have turned the world upside down are come hitherto also." I can readily think of several leading Christians today who would immediately file a motion of dis-association.

If what we intend to do as a result of this Consultation is merely a duplication or a little more of what is already being done, we put a seal of approval and integrity on what has failed up to now to really improve the lot of the dispossessed.

Dag Hammerskjöld in *Markings* states: "The great commitment is so much easier than the ordinary every day one — and can all too easily shut our hearts to the latter. A willingness to make ultimate sacrifice can be associated with and even produce a great hardness of heart". Certainly our basic elemental attitudes tend to regulate or influence even our most vaunted acts of benevolence.

Amidst the confusions and multiple visions of their destiny, the common people of this world, not being versed in theology, have need of workable formulae, tractible guide-posts for daily living. It is not prudent to take for granted that these are readily obtainable. They must be discovered afresh by each individual at both the spiritual and material levels, because "what gives life its value you can find and use but never possess".

In this great search, if we plumb the depths of intuition, we will discern the paramount conjunction of the instinct of survival and the supreme will to live. The spiritual dimension of Christianity in this is the imperative of mutuality of the group and the unity of its members. The cardinal mark of indentification of the Children of God is their bond of love which transcends the boundaries of race, colour, creed or culture. Under this conception, the family of God as a community of common interest has the unalterable task of praying, living and working for the establishment of the new order.

What one member does for another ought not to be based upon pity or charity. It should be done in instinctive response to the basic concern for the protection and survival of the whole family. The poverty and the disease of one member is the poverty and sickness of all. One for all and all for one.

Our duties as well as our rights proceed from the identical source. It is our bounteous and omnipresent Father who bestows that sanctity of personality which is inviolable and gives that liberty of person which is the inalienable obligation of every member of the family; and the equitable distribution of opportunity for development is an inseparable, indivisible element of our inherent morality. These are the preconditions (rather than the arguments of humanism) which hallow for us the proposition of social justice. The primal considerations may be taken for granted in the industrialized world, or they may be regarded as infantile, over-simplification of truth that does not apply to bare-faced reality in the impersonal relationship of our scientific age. But this is a cynicism that need not be exported.

Within this century, the so-called Third-World will probably embrace the majority of Christendom. It faces presently many specious but appealing options. It is daily offered attractive alternatives. In this Third World, it is still not too late in the light of its recent history to reassert in these modern times that the old-fashioned ideas and ideals of Christianity are eminently valid and eternally relevant. If the human race is to survive, it will only do so if it becomes in spirit and in truth the human family, concerned with the protection and survival of all its members. We can develop to our fullest potential if we undertake the task together in the love mutuality and trust that is possible if we become "the children of the Highest".

Purpose of the Consultation

by Eugene C. Blake

I am pleased to welcome the participants and guests who have come at the invitation of the World Council of Churches to this World Consultation on Ecumenical Assistance for Development Projects. We need and want your advice in determining the motivation, the structure, and the methods of the ecumenical contribution in relation to world development needs.

Since I have already used this word "development" twice in my first paragraph, (and it will be heard many times more in this short address) let me say how I use it. Perhaps we have used up the word since it already produces such negative emotional responses in so many quarters of the globe. The word development as used by the World Council of Churches never means simply a utopian unrealistic dream of materialistic fulfilment.

It refers rather to possible processes whereby the people of the whole world together may establish economic structures of sufficient justice and equality so that men may have a truly human life. We do not suppose that so-called underdeveloped nations should simply strive to copy the technological advances of the rich nations. Unless the life and goals of the "rich" nations are as radically changed in the process of world development as is the life of "poor" nations, the end of the process will clearly become more like hell on earth than like a heavenly utopia.

The essential thing in their opinion is to know whether we (developed countries) are ready to undertake the transformation of our society which will make the world more human, truly habitable by all mankind. If we are clear and resolute the technicians will be able to work out the appropriate solutions. But it is in our own mentality that first and most urgent conversion must take place.

A community of man, using the scientific knowledge and engineering techniques now available, but oriented toward a life that is good in a moral and spiritual sense is the concept towards which Christian development programmes must always aim.

In relation to Christians they ask us particularly: must we not be prophets and workers of that community and unity of all mankind if we are not to deny our faith?

Before I speak to you now on the significance and scope of this Consultation, I would like to present to you a brief historical perspective on the World Council of Churches' concern for development. The preoccupation of the ecumenical movement, both nationally and internationally, with development is not a new phenomenon although we did not formerly call it development. As early as the Life and Work Conference (Oxford 1937) the churches were expressing their concern for social-economic justice in a world perspective, but it was not until the Second Assembly of the World Council of Churches (Evanston 1954) and the commissioning of the Rapid Social Change Study that sustained attention was given to this crucial issue.

Partly of a result of the thinking done at the Church and Society Conference (Geneva 1966) and partly due to the increasing awareness of the "development issue" on the part of the churches, this concern became a major theme at the Fourth Assembly at Uppsala in 1968. The Assembly was also influenced by the report of the consultation at Beirut in April 1968, called by the Committee on Society, Development and Peace, jointly established by the Roman Catholic Church and the World Council of Churches. The Uppsala Assembly made a strong appeal to the member churches to participate in the efforts for world cooperation for development and gave a mandate to the World Council of Churches to pursue this concern. Many churches are responding or have responded.

Furthermore, the churches, through their missionary movements, have a long and impressive record of involvement in service and development projects. Service has been a major feature of Christian mission in developing countries since the late nineteenth century. Traditionally, the churches have been most active in education, medicine, and agriculture and a large measure of church resources to these programmes and projects have been channelled through mission agencies.

But what are the main aspects of the churches' present responsibility in the field of world development? This question has been a matter of study and discussion among churches on national and international levels. Judging from the reports of several such studies there seems to emerge a consensus that the churches' responsibility in this field should be directed to three major areas: education for development; efforts towards the establishment of social, economic and political structures conducive to development, on national and international levels; and direct programmes and services projects.

This Consultation is designed primarily to give attention to the third area, that is, the churches' concern for development projects. In this sense, this Consultation has a limited scope. Nevertheless, the *implications* of what you say on certain practical issues, and the *assumptions* on which you work will constantly bring in all the other questions.

The importance of this Conference has increased steadily since the idea of calling it arose, following the Uppsala Assembly in July 1968. Various churches were beginning to raise and commit relatively large sums for development and to launch campaigns in support of major giving for development as a concrete symbol of their Christian commitment. The main problem for the ecumenical movement seems to be to provide an efficient, well-planned, technically competent and ecumenically coordinated system for making the best use of these new funds and of the other continuing resources from mission and service agencies.

In recent months, however, the whole debate about Church sponsored development has entered a new and difficult phase. Our involvement in development projects is under serious questioning by those within the Church as well as concerned people outside the Church. Why should the churches be involved in development projects? Will not such involvement distort the main purpose and functions of the churches on the one hand and the goals and process of development on the other? Is it not adequate for the churches to confine their role to supporting projects sponsored by secular agencies, governments, inter-governmental organizations, etc. who in any case must carry the main responsibility for fostering development even as I have defined it? Is there any appropriate contribution that the churches can make in the field of development projects? If, as a result of this Conference, we can give any advice to our constituency and to the World Council of Churches which would help them to resolve these kinds of problems, we shall have accomplished a great deal indeed.

In this connection and as illustrations of the kind of problems we face, let me comment on three aspects or dimensions of the problem of Christian assistance for development which seem to be very real today: (a) our involvement in political issues and conflicts; (b) the ideological problem, and (c) the ecclesiological question.

I. The political dimension

A fundamental problem facing most of our churches in working for economic and social development is that they must cope with political pressures which may gravely influence if not distort their work. This seems to me as true for churches whether in the so-called "developed" or the "developing" countries. All our countries and regions have political interests which demand to be served. It is an illusion and, indeed in many respects, irresponsible to think that churches can or should live aloof from the political concerns and welfare of their people. This is evident for example in the efforts of the churches to be of assistance in the troubled areas of the Middle East and Nigeria.

The increase of the political factors in the whole development enterprise must make us both adventurous and wary: adventurous because this is our opportunity to demonstrate our concern for a larger human perspective, than one derived solely from national political goals and pressures; and wary because even the best of motives can be manipulated and exploited for quite other purposes.

The very nature of the ecumenical movement demands that it serve as a means of resisting the tendency of political considerations to over-power moral and spiritual goals. That is not to suggest that there is any one ecumenical answer or approach in a situation of political conflict. Certainly there is no "super Church perspective" on every difficult issue which can be cranked through the ecumenical computer on some kind of split second timing.

In this connection we need to give careful attention to the relation-ship between developed and developing countries or in this Con-ference more particularly between the donor and recipient agencies. There is a continuing tendency on the part of donors to impose their thinking, methodology, values and standards on developing countries by the very process of aidgiving. They have a great power of unilateral action because of their wealth. In our discussion at this Consultation on procedures and structures for ecumenical assistance to development projects, we should make every effort to avoid this danger. Representatives from the Third World must be given a major role in the decision-making processes at all levels. This is what ecumenical means.

II. The ideological factor

The hardest part of the discussion at this Consultation may centre around the ideological element in the debate about development. We were not called here specifically to discuss this problem, yet ideological assumptions about development always lie very near to the heart of any discussion of it. Several of our speakers will no doubt tell us about the way in which the development questions raise the ideological question: i. e. where the changes or lack of changes in the structures of society make "good" projects have an evil result. Hence a conference about new programmes of Church development can be frustrated because it must act on some assumption about which there is such a large and continuing debate.

The ideological problem is also difficult because, as with the political factor, there is no final answer to the debate. There are answers, and sometimes very contradictory answers. As in so many respects, we must operate as churches without absolute confidence that we know where we are going, or how to get there. We follow God's call in faith like Abraham "leaving home without knowing where he was going".

It is for this reason that I find the present so-called ideological debate about development increasingly unhelpful. This applies to both the traditional ideological debate about socialism and capitalism as well as the current debate among the reformists and revolutionaries. Over the last two decades the rigid absolutism of the parties in the traditional debate has softened considerably. The current ideological debate among revolutionaries, reformists and conservatives also has an air of unreality. All people are conservative about what they want to conserve and yet the same people can be very revolutionary about some other persons' structure, values, etc. What is not clear is the objective of revolutionary change, and the means of getting there. Of course, we all agree that many of our structures need change today but how much, and for what purpose and how shall the cost of the change be distributed? These are the kinds of questions which must surely trouble Christian development workers in every corner of the world.

In the current debate about the goals of development we have to consider what contribution we as Christians should make.

We must be open to ideas which may come from many religious, cultural, and ideological traditions. We should enter into this debate and make our contributions based on the Christian concepts of man and the Christian understanding of the quality of human life. We must prepare ourselves to *enunciate* these dynamic concepts more clearly, and *exemplify* them in our development programmes.

III. The ecclesiological factor

We must recognize that there are many people inside and outside the Church who still question the theological validity and the sociological relevance of the churches' involvement in development. This may be a question which for most of you at this Consultation is already answered, nevertheless for large numbers of sincere Christians our answers are either not very compelling or are in fact conflicting.

Despite the fact that most of the churches have a firm conviction about their rightful involvement in social justice they still in fact do not cooperate together in a common development programme. At this Consultation we should make a serious attempt to create a structure or structures which will facilitate the maximum cooperation of Christian agencies and churches — including those churches currently outside the membership of the World Council of Churches.

Is it not imperative for Christians to manifest their common witness in this crucial concern of our time? It should be recognized that the churches in the Socialist countries have certain practical difficulties in manifesting their concern for development through international ecumenical channels. This does not mean that they are not equally concerned or should not be concerned about world cooperation in development.

If we as churches have any particular claim to make it is that we are a world-wide community crossing national and racial barriers. Our involvement in development should enable us to manifest this characteristic of the Church and at the same time strengthen those factors in our current history which foster the realization of a just-world community. The fact that two-thirds of the world's family continues to suffer from injustice and under-development in a world of plenty is a moral outrage. The vision that beckons the churches to move forward in the concern for development is the vision of the one human family all of whose members have opportunity to live truly human lives and so as men to respond to the purposes of God.

Goals and Process of Development and Objectives for Development Projects

by Edward K. Hamilton

It seemed appropriate when I started to think about my remarks to begin with the quite accurate observation that I am virtually without qualifications to address a group of this kind. However, it then occurred to me that those responsible for selecting speakers may have relied on the fact that I have had the privilege during the past year of working closely with one of the towering public figures of our time, the Right Honourable Lester B. Pearson, who is rightly proud that he is the son and the grandson of Methodist ministers. If this explains my selection, it may be the first known case of innocence by association.

Nevertheless it is an honour to have this opportunity to set a few thoughts before you as you debate the role of the churches in the support of international development. If you find my musings too reflective of secular experience and criteria, I am sure you will filter them through your own experience and quickly sort out any which may be of use. As with most of the grand issues in human affairs, there are no fixed answers to the most fundamental questions in this field. There are only value judgements and hypotheses of varying degrees of probability.

My terms of reference relate to the topic "Goals and Process of Development and Objectives for Development Projects", but I have been given leave to interpret that title to include all of the questions being addressed in your various working groups. That is a dangerous invitation to extend to one of my garrulous tendencies. However, you will be relieved to know that I will confine myself to a few observations on two aspects of the problem you have gathered to discuss. First I will offer some thoughts on the process of development in the poor countries and the role of the churches in supporting it. Then I would like to ponder a bit the function of the churches with respect to public and governmental support for overseas development in the wealthy countries. If my treatment seems cursory and impressionistic, I plead the need for brevity; if it does not seem so, you may not be listening closely enough.

The question of goals for development is a vexing one indeed. Development is the term by which we refer to a particular kind of social change, which, if it yielded other results, we might otherwise designate by its most publicized symptoms — instability, partial disintegration, and in some cases even revolution. Most of the turmoil in history has not led to sustained improvement in living standards or in the quality of society or politics, nor has it been expected to, either by those who fomented it or still less by those who merely endured it. Most men in previous centuries have lived out their lives in dread of change. It is one of the novelties of our own age that change on a massive scale is not only expected but demanded by the great majority of human beings, and that, to be acceptable, it must promise to enlarge the total stock of economic and social advantages available to each polity. If the politics associated with this transformation are to be workable, it must also offer a credible prospect of providing enlarged portions of these advantages to most of the significant interest groups involved. Whether effective popular demand proceeds further to a truly egalitarian concept of distribution of the benefits of development varies with country — it can be persuasively argued that there are still many men behind many hoes to whom the concept of rapid development has no more relevance as the poet said than "the swing of Pleiades".

Nevertheless, it is clear nearly everywhere that what my fellow-countryman Harlan Cleveland first dubbed the "revolution of rising expectations" has assumed proportions of historic scale. It is with us wherever there is poverty, in rich countries as well as poor, it is irreversible, and it is growing. I shall not try you with the evidence for these conclusions; it is well-known and the consequences tolerably well-accepted. Those who argue — in the face of the facts — that events of the past decade have caused this tide to recede in the face of a contravening revolution of disillusion remain few and unpersuasive.

Indeed, we are nearing a point where the economic aspects of development occupy the same position in the theories of governance operating in poor countries which life itself occupies in most Western philosophy. That is, economic development is becoming less a goal among other goals than a ground of being without which other goals become meaningless. It is a prime object of national life, a fundamental measure of societal success, and the universal political platform upon which leadership — democratic or authoritarian — is often chosen and nearly always judged.

This ascendancy has made of economic development an identifiable academic discipline centered around a similarly distinct area of public policy in the councils of both rich and poor and in the international organizations. It has developed its own language — a patois often seeming to consist largely of equal parts obscure acronym and social science jargon — and it has generated its own relatively small but active band of *literati*. Within this group mutual education and empathy have multiplied manyfold and the body of knowledge has grown apace. It seems safe to suggest that an overwhelming fraction of the scholars and practitioners who have ever enjoyed much systematic knowledge of the mechanics of economic growth are alive today and belong to this elite.

The incessant production of new data, new hypotheses, and new methods — and their rapid dissemination among an ever more alert and accomplished cadre of policy-makers in the developing countries — is one of the most encouraging elements of the present scene.

However, the very explosion of knowledge, along with a number of other less pleasant explosions, has thrown into relief the undoubted fact that there is a great deal more to development than economics. It is this "discovery" and its aftermath which prompts my first attempt at counsel to you as you deliberate the role of the churches. Offered with true Polonian presumptuousness, it consists of four related injunctions:

1. Do not delay action pending a "general theory" of development which incorporates political, social, and spiritual objectives and effects.

2. Distinguish sharply between study of the ends and means of development designed to increase knowledge, and establishment of goals and methods in any real-world situation; accept that the latter must largely be done by the government of the developing country involved, working with donor governments and international organizations.

3. Expect much higher levels of sensitivity to outside prescription and much slower progress toward consensus on goals and methods in the non-economic spheres.

4. Do not attempt to avoid the steps necessary to become competent to join in and criticize debate about development policy, both economic and social.

I. The first injunction seems at first blush akin to the title of a popular recent book in the United States, *Please Don't Eat the Daisies*. It would have seemed wildly implausible only a few years ago that there would be any tendency among sensible men to halt efforts to raise incomes in the desperately poor two-thirds of the world until guided by a formula for social engineering which, as it were, effs the ineffable. Yet today — even in the generally excellent background papers prepared for your use — one finds the explicit or implicit suggestion that although economic development programmes may raise incomes we know so little of the side effects that they may be doing more harm than good when damage to political and social structures and spiritual values is taken into account. This is a theme of increasing strength in my own country where there is an active search among many erstwhile internationalists for reasons for disengagement from world affairs.

The idea is now solemnly advanced, at least in private, that development cooperation should cease until we have scientific proof of the correlation between types and rates of economic change on the one hand and other kinds of change on the other. That is, we should do no more until, for example, we *know* with reasonable precision whether export-led growth at six percent will help or hinder the evolution of democratic institutions, how it will affect tribal loyalties, or what it will do to the individual's conception of himself and his Creator. The supposed *coup de grace* of this case is that the present plight of the "developed" countries, wallowing in their own polluted juices, is hardly something to be aspired to.

I hardly need to say that I find this position unpersuasive in the extreme. My disagreement begins with the implicit premise that the wealthy are authorized and equipped to decide what the goals of developing countries should be — what is "good" for them. My own notion is that this choice is and must be entirely in the hands of the developing countries, with the sole reservation that willingness to cooperate through transfer of resources should confer upon aid donors the right to be informed and to receive a fair hearing when decisions are made. To my mind our best efforts in the 1970's, including those of the churches, should be devoted to creating the global system of multilaterally-controlled programming mechanisms within developing countries which are necessary to this joint process. This would not, however, change the locus of power and responsibility to make basic decisions about goals. This would remain in the hands of local authorities, the overwhelming majority of which have opted strongly for economic growth, while at the same time doing the best they can to learn about and control the side effects. I think we should respect and support that decision.

With respect to the technical side of the issue, an officer of a social science research organization is not given to understating the potential of social science research, but he also, I would hope, recognizes its limitations. Few are more ardent in support of research into the non-economic facets of development than I. Contrary to popular belief, even most economists are not oblivious to these spheres, they simply recognise that they are even more subjective and difficult than economics. There is already a large body of research literature on the relation between economic and political development. Projects addressed to the social, anthropological, ecological, and psychological dimensions are rather fewer in number, but expanding rapidly. All these efforts together, I think the participants would agree, represent the most tentative gropings into some of the darkest and most labyrinthine passages of social research. They deserve to be supported, multiplied in number, and vastly increased in scope. Yet, whatever the scale of expansion, it seems clear that a general theory of development, if feasible at all, will require data, methods, and capacity to synthesize which do not exist nor promise to exist for some decades.

At our present stage the net effect of new data in non-economic areas is to deepen the theoretical quandary, not to point out reliable solutions. One ever more frequent consequence is the conclusion that there are no truly developed countries in the world. This is certainly true in many ways, but there is a breathtaking arrogance — not to say cruelty — to extending this argument to the proposition that efforts to raise income should be deferred until the rest of us have defined, and presumably achieved, "real" development. Our difficulties in choosing which of our two cars to take along which paved road to which air-conditioned building to do which well-paid job in which thriving productive sector may have so distorted our senses that we are now afflicted by a kind of moral blindness to the plight of the truly disadvantaged. Arrogance is compounded by the implicit assumption that the developing countries must repeat all of our mistakes. But the death blow to this position is the utter certainty that even if we, the disgruntled wealthy, were prepared to tolerate delay, the developing countries are not. They intend to move ahead, learning as much as they can while doing as much as they can. The question — and it may be decisive — is whether the rest of us are prepared to help.

If we are so prepared, it follows that both foreign governments and foreign-based churches — for the two often look much the same to a non-Christian developing country — would do well to avoid settled positions in the theoretical debate, to accept the goals and priorities determined by each developing country after due consultation, and to direct their attention to the operational questions of means. If a man's or a government's philosophy on the cosmic questions permits of any positive action, I think you will find it remarkable how much agreement can be reached on such practical matters as a road, a bridge, a school, a water supply system, a disease eradication programme, an import policy or even a tax system. Outsiders of all stripes minimize the political disadvantages of their participation in delicate deliberations, and maximize their contribution to positive progress, by restricting their roles to the programmatic debate where talk is disciplined by the need for action.

II. This train of thought leads directly into the basis for my second injunction which makes explicit that those of us outside the developing countries must accept, indeed rejoice in the fact that judgments on goals will be in the increasingly capable hands of the developing countries themselves. I repeat myself on this point because there is some evidence that it has yet to penetrate in some quarters. There remain a few countries in the world which do not have even the most primitive facilities to develop goals for the mobilization and allocation of resources, but they are fast declining in number. Increasingly, serious involvement in decision processes entails living with the problem and the decision-makers in the developing country. No longer can one hope to programme aid largely from Washington, New York, Paris, Geneva or Moscow.

Similarly, no longer can any donor — or at least any donor not providing a very large fraction of import finance — hope to impose choices of strategy or tactics according to his own ideology or interests. Developing countries increasingly know their own minds in these vital matters. They are susceptible to rational argument, particularly technical argument, but not to direction based on supposed higher theological or other wisdom. Thus, although it is natural and necessary to debate the theological basis of a church role in development support, it is important not to confuse this with the basis upon which goals will be established in the process itself. The authors of your background papers are quite correct, in my judgment, to point out that theology offers little if any basis for operational choice in this field. But I would go further to suggest that even if it did, the churches must reconcile themselves to a supporting role on a stage dominated by governments. However, it can still be, as I will suggest, a vital role.

III. The third injunction suggests that in this programming process, the churches and all other outsiders must also accept the fact that agreement on non-economic goals and means will require much more time and patience on both sides of the table than those in the economic sphere. This is often a bitter pill to swallow for basic values are usually at stake. A true humanitarian is just as worried about income distribution as he is about income levels. A support of western democracy finds it difficult to accept a political system which permits only one party and abridges some personal freedoms. An admirer of the lovely traditions imbedded in the ancient cultures of developing countries is reluctant to see them sacrificed to values which he, as a result of his own experience, believes to be unworthy and unnecessary to development.

These concerns are just as legitimate as those more narrowly economic in character, but as realists we must recognize that they are in a different and more delicate *political* category. If clumsily inserted into the development dialogue, they can make impossible cooperation to any end. In any case, they move the dialogue closer to the white heat of nationalist fervour which co-exists in most developing coutries with a strong desire for economic assistance. This separation of non-economic matters is artificial, imprecise, and subject to change with the rise and fall of demagogues, but few would doubt that it is present and of urgent significance to understanding the politics of the aid relationship.

We have, then, what a systems analyst calls a tradeoff. Movement to introduce non-economic elements into the factors by which development performance is judged — and on which the Pearson Commission argues that development aid should in future be largely conditioned — offers great potential advantages but perhaps even greater risks of dissolving the whole basis for joint action by rich and poor.

I would caution against any rigid rules in this matter; each new field of effort in which criteria may be evolved should be considered on its merits in the light of the nature of the dialogue in each country. However, my own concept of the development process suggests a strong presumption against adventurous risks of derailing economic cooperation unless the excesses practised or permitted by local authorities approach a barbarism which no civilized values can survive. This is not the same thing as a ban on non-economic development criteria, though some thoughtful men would urge this. Rather, it is a plea for extreme caution in introducing such criteria, caution which takes account of the different order of sensitivity they will almost everywhere encounter, and which is rooted in reasonable confidence that rapid increases in income will encourage the humanist yeast in the society which is the best long-run hope for popular government attending to all of its responsibilities to all of its citizens.

Of course, the greatest difficulties come with the borderline cases — those aspects of public policy which straddle social and economic policy with major implications for both, as well as for politics. The most important of these is population policy and I would be less than honest if I failed to face this dilemma directly.

You do not need to be reminded of the significance of this problem and the difficulties associated with it. It would be much easier all around if we could ignore it in return for some moderate loss of efficiency or speed in the development effort. However, in my judgment the issues are too central and too much a source of potential disaster to allow that course. The stark fact is that failure to take effective measures to prevent unwanted children can drown all the progress any development programme achieves. Not all of this danger follows from the strictly economic logic of resources and their uses; much of it reflects the political and psychological effects of teeming, idle and largely urban masses. But I would suggest that in most large developing countries, including most of those who are persuaded that they have no population problem, the economic implications alone establish an inescapable responsibility for both donor and recipient in an aid relationship to make family planning a prominent and equal element in any schedule of development goals and criteria.

IV. To focus on this highly sensitive aspect of socio-economic policy is to dramatize the importance of the fourth injunction. In matters of population policy, as in all other areas of the development dialogue, rapidly increasing sophistication now imposes a severe "knowledge test" on the would-be participant. Put more bluntly, a significant role in the development process now requires the outsider to know in great and technical detail what he is talking about. This obviously does not mean he must be right in every case; none of us can aspire to that sainted state. It does mean that the foreigner must command a working knowledge of the past and present state of the economy in question, the political and other constraints upon action, and the specific problems raised by the effects — including indirect effects — of the projects or measures under consideration.

Several points follow from this premise. The first is that the *operational* goals for projects and programmes must almost invariably be expressed and adopted at the level of a single country. However the Federalists among us may lament it — and I share many of their regrets — the nation-state will be with us for quite some time yet and will be the political and economic universe in which goals and policies are most authoritatively debated and determined. Each has and will have its own peculiar structure of interests and principles, and almost none will be sufficiently similar to any other that one can assume identical potential and procedure where development is concerned.

Let me emphasize that this is not a bar to regional or sub-regional cooperation among developing countries, which should be encouraged to the limits of our abilities. However, the real world will correspond more closely to our conception of it if we keep firmly in mind that the decisions governing the nature and extent of regional cooperation, and the great bulk of the capacity to implement agreed plans and programmes will remain in the control of national authorities. The first task in development is to persuade national governments that action, unilateral or cooperative, is required; and all parties must accept that this decision, as well as the assessment of prospective benefits and actual results, will be considered largely in a context of national priorities and feasibilities. That this does not foreclose cooperation among neighbours even where one country must make greater concession because of its more advanced economic state is amply demonstrated by the enlightened policy of Kenya in the formation of the East African Economic Community.

I also do not mean here to discredit global goals for overall economic progress in the developing world. The Pearson Commission suggested a global growth target, which is related to the one just agreed upon by Professor Tinbergen's United Nations Development Planning Committee. These targets, and that which the UN General Assembly seems likely to accept for the Second Development Decade, call for average growth in the Gross National Product (GNP) of poor countries of the order of 6—7 % per year. This is an ambitious goal and a useful one because it lends specificity to the aims around which the world community can organize. But it is important to remember that it tells the operator almost nothing about the proper goal in a particular country. The global target is an average of well over one hundred countries, some of which will be far above it and others well below. Targets which guide specific programmes must reflect the individual possibilities in the relevant country, whether that means six per cent per year or nine per cent or even five per cent.

The targets do, however, have the added value of making it clear that concern about the welfare of the poor countries must extend beyond the dramatic and heart-rending symptoms of underdevelopment to the infinitely complex process of growth itself. No source of substantial development support, public or private, can limit its vision or its resources to short-term feeding or clothing or vaccination programmes, valuable and popular as these activities are. To be serious — and, I would argue, to be persuasive to electorates and congregations increasingly sophisticated about poverty — one must enter the often bewildering jungle of economic data, criteria, and appraisal. One must form some basis for judgments on the technical questions posed and, even more important, he must convey the nature and importance of those judgments to his constituency, which, it is usually safe to predict, will be less than enthralled by the topic upon first hearing.

The requirement most basic to this role is the need for a permanent mission in the developing countries where substantial programmes are undertaken. Broadly speaking, there are two kinds of organizations in the business of international development: those with field missions and those which depend on those with field missions. The churches, taken together, would seem to be a large enough potential source of support to become one of the former. It is extremely important, for reasons of both efficiency and politics, that any such missions be ecumenical in character and divorced from proselytizing and other parochial activities. The churches need this combination of constraint and protection almost as much as governments need a multilateral framework.

However, it would be a great boon to the development effort if the great churches of the West demonstrated their determination to enter the development field in a serious way by establishing central field missions. Properly designed, financed, and staffed, these could be responsible for conceiving and preparing development projects, negotiating with hosts and collaborators, evaluating results, and advising the constituent confessions with respect to both past and future. This is not, I must emphasize, a task for ordinary priests, ministers, or missionaries, however valuable they are to their parishioners and may be to the programmes which are undertaken as a result. Nor is it a system which can afford to be responsive to most of the highly localized requests for support from individual congregations in developing countries. Let me also be clear that this kind of mission would not have and should not expect to have negotiating weight comparable to the governments which will continue to be the major sources of aid.

Nevertheless, an ecumenical mission, in addition to its beneficial effect on the volume of church aid and on the rationality with which it is provided and distributed, could perform the extremely important role of an informed, pro-development critic of official programmes. In my opinion this function is now badly needed and largely unperformed with respect to most developing countries. Governments always have much on their minds besides development. International organizations can do some finger-pointing, but their destinies are too closely tied to the favour of governments to permit complete candour. The churches, if properly equipped, could become a strong voice for development and an equally strong alarm device when will falters or is diverted to other ends. In some wealthy countries — though not regretfully, in my own — the churches have already made a good start toward this role. If they can equip themselves to speak the language of the policy-maker, to be familiar with the issues which must shape his judgment, and to make known their views in a timely fashion, development might less often be lost in the welter of conflicting national policy objectives in both rich countries and poor.

This brings me to my second and final topic, the role of the churches with respect to public knowledge of and support for development in wealthy countries. The importance of this question is obvious. The efforts of the churches and other private groups are important but they will mean little unless and until there is a recrudescence of will to support development and a corresponding expansion in the flow of concessional, official aid from rich countries to poor. This flow, which stood at $ 6,4 billion from non-Communist countries in 1968, is not growing with the Gross National Products in the industrialized world. It is shrinking, largely because of negative trends in the United States. This is easily the most serious challenge and opportunity on the current scene for all who find development important.

It is difficult to generalize about the current role of the churches in this regard because it varies so greatly from country to country. In some countries in Europe and North America, the churches are a powerful, if sometimes lightly informed, force for development and development aid. In others, including my own, overseas development is a new and too often ignored area of their concern. There has been more movement to correct this in the past two years than in all the years before, but I think it is fair to say that the level of interest and knowledge on development matters is still well below the critical threshold at which ordinary ministers and members of congregations could be expected to become seized with these issues and moved into action.

This is a big subject and I want to limit myself to two focal points. The first is the need for the churches to take in hand and try to make more actionable the humanitarian case for development aid. The paradox of the present is that, while the elements of human experience which reinforce the sense of communal responsibility for a minimal level of individual welfare are getting stronger, the humanitarian case for aid in particular kinds and amounts — which are the really difficult issues — is probably getting weaker in the United States and perhaps in other major donor countries. The main reasons are three:

1. Humanitarian arguments are inherently difficult to translate into operational steps. (How large a step toward decency this year?)

2. Growing domestic difficulties implicitly (and now sometimes explicitly) argue that humanitarianism must begin and end at home.

3. It is impossible to promise achievement of "decency" by American or European standards in many large low-income countries within our lifetimes at any level of aid thus far seriously contemplated.

It is important to recognize that these problems cannot be dismissed or ignored if humanitarian concerns are to have impact on the central questions in the aid debate which, I repeat, are not so much concerned with whether there will be aid, but with how much, to whom, and according to what criteria. There are powerful responses to each of the three, but the churches have not yet mounted a systematic and world-wide attempt to develop and disseminate them. Where, for example, is an attempt to provide backing for clear, partially quantitative definitions of decency which might be used as standards in discussing goals in both high and low-income countries? Where is an attempt to define a decent *rate* of progress in order to focus attention on the dynamics of change in the poor countries rather than on the point at which they will begin to resemble Switzerland? Where is an attempt to link the problems of domestic and international poverty into the same pattern of human responsibility and effort? And, if it is justified, where is the pressure for vastly multiplied aid flows to multiply the rate of progress and shorten the period of planetary imbalance?

These are some of the questions to which the guardians of morality in our societies must address themselves if they hope to translate principles more perfectly into practice.

My other focus is the possible role of the churches in persuading governments to organize themselves under multilateral auspices to mount the new campaign for development cooperation which the Pearson Commission, the Tinbergen Committee, and most other authorities have concluded is imperative. The churches of the world can, through their distinguished world leaders, lend great force and drama to appeals for government action. This appeal is multiplied if it is made in unison. At the risk of immodesty, I would invite your attention to at least one suggestion in the Pearson Report which might merit this kind of attention.

This is the recommendation that the international aid authorities convene a conference sometime this year to consider creation of improved machinery to perform the four major functions necessary to a new resurgence of development cooperation: (i) assessment of development performance; (ii) estimation of aid requirements; (iii) coordination of aid with other resource flows and policies crucial to development, and (iv) review donor performance on their development commitments. The conference should include the relevant international organizations, including those concerned with trade and capital movements, at least the major aid donors, and appropriate representatives of the aid recipients. It must be a fairly small group it if is to move ahead with reasonable dispatch, but it must be so structured that all major interests are represented.

In my opinion the convening and success of this conference is critical not only to the internal workings of the aid effort, but to the public attitude toward development as well. The American public, for one, will not support development aid until it understands the need for it and the machinery established to meet the need. The churches could, if they chose, contribute to meeting this test.

I have rambled on a bit longer than I should so I shall be very brief in closing. We hear a great deal about "relevance" in these times. The meaning of the term varies with its user but it most commonly denotes the degree to which men and institutions grapple with the massive injustice and imbalance in the world which has accompanied a century of unbroken technological revolution. My own litmus of relevance is deeply sensitive to concern and willingness to address the problem of reducing poverty in the world as the first responsibility of humanity. Your interest and that of the churches in this problem is amply evidenced by this meeting and by the most encouraging progress of SODEPAX in the form of the Joint Programme on World Development of the World Council of Churches and the Pontifical Commission Justice and Peace. I applaud your determination and urge you to even greater efforts in the future. Those of us engaged in this effort may hope to fulfil the dictum of one of my country's most famous jurists who, having defined life as "action and passion", observed that "it is required of a man that he should share the passion and action of his time at peril of being judged not to have lived".

Goals and Process of Development and Objectives of Development Projects

by S. L. Parmar

I

This paper does not discuss specific issues of development such as capital formation, role of government and private enterprise, population planning, trade and aid questions and so on. That makes it both sketchy and limited in scope. My intention is to suggest a possible perspective from which developmental efforts at national and international levels and at the more modest level of ecumenically assisted projects, may be viewed.

There is one major point in the whole presentation. Social justice is emphasised as the over-arching goal of development within which the two other important goals that have been mentioned, namely, economic growth and self-reliance should be integrated.

Development projects have validity only within the larger framework of national development programmes. Therefore, in order to determine their place and role it is necessary to consider some aspects pertaining to goals and process of development.

II

In a fundamental sense, the central goal of development may be called "self-development". Up to a point this would correspond to the concept of self-sustaining growth or self-reliance. But these are essentially economic concepts. Self-reliance means the ability of a country to maintain a desired rate of growth through its own resources. Its savings should suffice to meet its investment needs. A part of such savings is converted into exports to fetch enough foreign exchange to finance current imports and debt obligations. Hence such a condition indicates a freedom from foreign loans or grants.

Self-reliance does not mean self-sufficiency. Trade and investment continue to have significant roles in development. But through them the economy should be helped to acquire sufficient productive power and savings capacity to meet its international obligations. Obviously a high rate of growth in national and per capita incomes is essential for achieving the goal of self-reliance.

But self-development does not mean only a high rate of growth. It also implies a more equitable distribution of resources and economic power, and new relationships between social groups, so that development of one does not depend upon or lead to deprivation of the other. A high rate of growth could go with exploitation of the many by the few, as was the experience of today's industrial nations in their pre-development period. Not only was there a pauperisation of the proletariat within the country, (England, France, Germany, even USA) by a handful of owners of means of production, but there was also an extension of such exploitation to other nations in the form of colonialism. While developing nations have neither the possibility nor the inclination, and certainly not the power to embark on colonialism to sustain their economic progress, they can, and sometimes do, pursue exploitative policies domestically and have a fair rate of growth. In some erstwhile colonies, it is being said that we have exchanged foreign imperialism for "domestic imperialism". A few of these nations have even shown better economic performance than many other developing nations. Clearly, such a situation could not be described as "self-development". Social justice reflected in greater equality of opportunity, a more egalitarian social order, a diffusion of economic and political power from the few to the many, is the most important element of self-development.

Thus social justice incorporates equality and human dignity. These are non-quantifiable entities, hence they tend to be ignored or played down by social scientists. We often operate with the approach that if something cannot be quantified it is not very important. Rather a strange attitude considering how important such non-quantifiable concepts as patriotism, nationalism, enlightened self-interest, etc., are recognised to be.

Underprivileged groups like scheduled castes and scheduled tribes in India, have received large economic benefits since independence. Their social and economic progress is most striking in comparison to other groups. But old prejudices persist and discrimination takes new forms. Some of my students from these groups (specially the first) who occupy high positions in our administrative set-up have said, with tears in their eyes: "What good is economic betterment without social equality and human dignity." One could see similar elements in the black revolution in the USA. It is a struggle for a better economic deal no doubt, but more fundamentally for human dignity.

We could then interpret the central goal of development to consist of three inter-related objectives: economic growth, self-reliance and social justice. It is submitted that primacy should be accorded to social justice not simply on ethical grounds but in order to ensure a high rate of growth over time, and a steady progression towards self-reliance. This would be different from the generally prevalent approach in which rate of growth is singled out as the most important goal of development.

III

Economic growth, by which is meant a steady rise in the standard of living, is vital for developing countries. Pressure of population, massive poverty, rising expectations, the fact that political consciousness has preceded economic ability to meet aspirations, etc., make rapid economic growth an imperative. It is rightly said that we must run even in order to stand still, and if we wish to progress, we must take big leaps. Consequently, the rate of growth becomes more important than the fact of growth.

There are however a number of problems with this approach. First, it reduces development to a purely economic phenomenon. Second, it assumes that injection of sufficient resources like capital, technique, etc., will by itself bring about development. This is too much of a *laissez-faire* approach in relation to the situation in developing countries. Resources can give results only if adequate institutions are set up for utilising them. If all this is to be done quickly, it calls for radical structural changes. Gradualism will not do.

Third, it presents a yardstick for measuring development that dooms most developing countries to permanent poverty. According to certain projections, in the year 2000, India (even if it achieves a $+ 5 \%$ annual rate of growth) will be poorer in comparison to developed nations than it is today. The present 1 : 60 ratio in per capita incomes of India and USA may then be in the region of 1:100. Instead of catching up we will be stumbling far behind. It almost amounts to saying that the harder a nation works the poorer it will be in a relative sense. Knowing this, it would be suicidal for us to make economic growth the only measure of progress. Perhaps the preoccupation with the widening gap between rich and poor nations has to be given up. Each developing nation is really competing with itself. Its present performance should be an improvement upon its earlier performance. In the process, if it comes nearer to developed nations, well and good, but even if it seems to lag behind, that should not be taken as lack of achievement. Due to the large technological and demographic gaps it is almost certain that the distance between developed and developing nations will remain and even widen for a long time to come. We have, therefore, to evolve a concept of development which will give us a sense of equality and dignity even with relative poverty.

Fourth, one finds that in many countries of the Third World a satisfactory rate of growth has not contributed to the stability and well-being of the nation. That shows that people are seeking something more than statistical evidence of progress.

IV

As one looks at the contemporary scene in the Third World, it seems that political problems have assumed greater importance than economic ones. After three Five Year Plans, India has made only marginal dents in her massive poverty. Unemployment, rising prices, debt obligation, deficits in balance of payments and demographic burdens continue to plague the economy. If concerted efforts are necessary to deal with these problems the need for economic planning is greater, not less. And yet we have been forced to have a plan holiday. The Fourth Plan, which should have commenced in 1966, has yet to be launched. Incorrigible denigrators of planning would ascribe our misfortunes to planning itself, and suggest the panacea of private enterprise. But they should not forget that over the last two decades the Indian economy has achieved a creditable growth rate, which could never have been possible without planned effort. And yet instability grows.

The upheavals witnessed in Pakistan in mid-1969 show that it is in a similar predicament. During the sixties Pakistan had a higher rate of growth than most Asian countries, excepting Taiwan and S. Korea. Similarly, Nigeria, Kenya, Indonesia, Malaysia, Brazil, to mention a few other developing countries, provide instances of fair rates of growth and instability going together. It is not intended to suggest that lack of social justice is the only cause of upheavals in many developing nations. There are a variety of causes. But if one goes to the root of the matter, it would be seen that many of these struggles even though they take ethnic, tribal, cultural and linguistic forms, constitute a part of the quest for equality and human dignity.

Much is heard these days about the green revolution in India. Experts agree that a significant breakthrough in agricultural productivity has taken place. This has eased the grim food situation which our country faced three years ago. It is true that some of the improvement is due to favourable monsoons. But technical factors such as irrigation, use of fertilisers and miracle seeds, new techniques, etc., are responsible for the improvement. And yet fears are being expressed by responsible government spokesmen that the green revolution will change into a red revolution unless we pursue policies of social justice and reduce existing economic and social inequalities.

In a note submitted to the Economic and Social Council's Commission on Social Development about a fortnight ago, UN Secretary General, U Thant, raised some questions about the green revolution. He warned developing countries that unless they introduce land reforms they are likely to face grave trouble. While recognising the striking improvement in agricultural production he points to the social problems that have come in its wake. He is, therefore, somewhat pessimistic about the green revolution in the way it is implemented in countries like India.

According to U Thant: "The green revolution is likely to benefit primarily those farmers who are already engaged in commercial production rather than subsistence farmers, and among commercial farmers, big ones more than small producers... There is a distinct possibility that small farmers may gradually be squeezed out of the market by big producers and that tenants may be evicted."

Similar concern was expressed by India's Food and Agricultural Minister last December. He said: "There has been a breakthrough in agriculture. Arrangement for public allocation of inputs and credits

45

have considerably improved. But the beneficiaries are not those who are living on a pittance of a few rupees a month, but the privileged minority of substantial and middle cultivators. With 47 % of farm families owning only one acre of land and 22 % having no land at all, with only 3 to 4 % of big cultivators enjoying all power, wielding all influence, making all decisions in collaboration with the governmental machinery, and appropriating to themselves all the skill, the resources, the expertise governmental agencies offer, the poor half of the villages have little to thank anybody for."

Analysing the situation, an Indian weekly (LINK, January 18, 1970) says: "As a result of the green revolution, a section of rich people are rapaciously pushing into the rural areas. These are big monopoly capitalists, businessmen, retired top officers of the armed forces, contractors, etc. With immense resources at their disposal and the attraction of big profits, these sections are ruthlessly evicting or squeezing out small holders and tenants."

It is becoming clear that the green revolution has fermented agrarian unrest. An official study of the Home Ministry on "The causes and nature of current agrarian tensions" gives two possible reasons why the green revolution has become another weapon of social oppression instead of an instrument of social transformation. First the outmoded agrarian social structure and second the fact that the new technology and strategy have been geared to the goals of production to the neglect of social imperatives. Consequently, disparity, instability and unrest are growing.

The aforementioned article in LINK quotes Gunnar Myrdal, who observed that the Indian village is "like a complex molecule among whose parts extreme tensions have been built up. Although the tensions criss-cross in a manner that maintains equilibrium, it is conceivable that they might reorganise in a way that would explode the molecules. This probably would not happen spontaneously, but as a result of a forceful onslaught from outside," and suggests that the green revolution as it is now directed seems to provide the outside hammering to explode the molecule. That may have been the thought in the mind of the Home Minister when he said that "unless the green revolution is accompanied by a revolution based on social justice, I am afraid the green revolution may not remain green".

46

Therefore, while recognising the importance of rate of growth and self-reliance as objectives of development, it is suggested that the framework in which these should be attempted should be that of social justice. Only then will the overall goal of "self-development" be possible.

V

The most important component of social justice is a just distribution of national product, i. e. distributive justice. It is often argued that pursuit of welfare and distributive justice will slow down the rate of growth. That is why a preoccupation with the latter seeks a postponement of egalitarian economic policies. Let us see if there is any justification in such an approach.

Welfare measures in the field of health and sanitation have brought down the death rate sharply in most developing countries. Even with a constant or slightly reduced birth rate, population is increasing at a much faster rate than before, necessitating larger demographic investments. A substantial portion of increased national product is diverted to the maintenance of additions to population and cannot, therefore, be used for productive investment that would accelerate the rate of growth. Welfare almost becomes a brake on development.

This may appear to be so from a narrow point of view. But if we take a nation's long-term interest, as we should in discussions of development, an improvement in the health of the people improves the quality and productivity of human resources. It also subscribes to the tenets of social justice by providing facilities to a group which is unable to do so for itself.

Welfare measures also involve a transference of resources from the higher income group to the lower income group. This is sometimes described as a shift of income from the traditionally saving group to the traditionally non-saving group. As such it slows down the rate of capital formation and consequently the rate of growth. From this, it is argued that policies of distributive justice should be postponed till such time as self-sustaining growth has been achieved. My submission is that without pursuing policies based on social and economic justice, it is impossible to reach self-sustaining growth.

The above type of argument has many flaws. One, it operates with a static concept of saving and non-saving groups. Two, if investment efforts of the so-called saving groups were really effective the problem of production should have been solved by now, and we should have been in a position to introduce a better distribution of national income. That it is not so shows that the savings efforts of the traditionally saving class are inadequate. Three, this approach ignores the role of government in mobilising savings through taxation, consumption regulation, public borrowing and deficit financing. In developing countries it is not possible to meet the investment requirements demanded by a high rate of growth through voluntary savings, therefore, forced saving becomes essential for our economies. Four, distributive justice is the first step in building up the production and saving capacity of erstwhile non-saving groups.

The experience of developed nations provides a helpful parallel at this point. In the early stages of their development savings were not voluntarily coming forth through the free play of market forces, although this is a cherished myth. Savings were forced from the economy. Some of it was squeezed from the working class and the peasantry in the form of surplus value. One may disagree with the theoretical ramifications of Marx's theory of surplus value, but he was right in showing that the owners of means of production built up their savings by exploiting labour. Forced savings thus become a common feature in the pre-development experience of today's industrial nations, and the present experience of developing nations. But there the similarity ends. Developed nations forced savings from those who had less capacity to save; the policy of distributive justice suggested for developing countries would force savings from those who have the greatest ability to save and in the process build up the saving potential of the less privileged groups.

Two phrases are often heard when the "growth versus distribution" bogey is raised. First, "you cannot distribute poverty". Second, "production first then distribution". If these were valid the primacy of social justice as a goal of development could not be maintained. Therefore, it is necessary to take a closer look at such popular notions.

It sounds plausible to say that poverty cannot be distributed. But a nation can certainly distribute what it has. If that happens to be

48

poverty, one must begin with that. Second, such an argument clouds the real issue. It is not poverty which is to be distributed but riches which exist within an overall situation of poverty. The process of welfare and distributive justice takes from those who have more and will continue to have more relatively to others even after such deductions. Third, in most of the developing countries we witness a repugnant situation of islands of affluence surrounded by unrelieved poverty. This is a result of existing patterns of distribution of economic and political power. At the end of three Five Year Plans economic inequalities have increased in India. A vicious circle of this kind can be broken only by more equitable distribution. Otherwise, even when the few rich continue to grow richer, they can still say: "you cannot distribute poverty", because the nation as a whole will be poor. Fourth, distributive justice is important from the point of view of efficient use of resources. We all recognise that underfed people cannot work efficiently, hence they are unable to make full contribution to social production, but the same holds true for overfed people. Both conditions are unhealthy and weaken productive capacity. The economy as a whole should function more efficiently if the overfed have less and the underfed more and both are restored to health. And yet we have the strange spectacle of economic policies that favour the better off sections more in the name of "incentives", and neglect or even deprive the weaker sections in the name of "sacrifices necessary for development".

Fifth, the slogan "production first then distribution" is a clever smokescreen for perpetuating social injustice and power of the possessing classes. If these groups resist redistribution of resources today, does it not stand to reason that when production has increased they will resist redistribution even more? Because then their economic and political power will have increased and they will have more to lose under policies of equitable distribution.

Sixth, it is also not clear at which level of production we begin to say that now we have enough to start redistributing. As mentioned before, most developing nations will be relatively poorer in comparison to developed nations by the year 2000. It would then be said that we must postpone distributive justice till we have produced enough to narrow the gap between rich and poor countries.

Seventh, there would be some justification in leaving resources in the control of better off sections in developing countries, if these groups followed austerity to maximise the savings ratio, and thereafter invested resources according to national priorities. But the behaviour of these groups has been rather different so far. Generally they indulge in conspicuous consumption which is a waste of resources in economies of scarcity. An unfortunate consequence is the demonstration effect of consumption patterns of the elite; it distorts consumption in general and tempts the low income groups to follow suit. In traditional economies one of the problems is the high propensity for social consumption — on ceremonies, festivals, etc. This is evident from the present pattern in Indian villages. Increased agricultural production and rise in incomes have caused a spurt in wasteful consumption, thus reducing resources for new investments. Theoretically one could make out a case for no ceiling on incomes, provided it was assisting the process of capital formation. If this does not happen in practice, one could still allow high incomes but ensure savings by imposing curbs on consumption. That would, in effect, become a way of redistributing real resources of the country.

Eighth, from the experience of developed nations it is proved that welfare policies contribute to increased production over time, and also ensure better balance between different sectors of the economy. Price support policies, agricultural subsidies, unemployment insurance, etc., are examples. These illustrate a process of more equitable distribution of resources by taking from those with ability for the sake of those with need. Welfare is not a leakage of national resources but a contributor to productive capacity.

In the light of the above we have to recast our views about incentive, property, etc. Usually when we talk of incentives we are thinking of special encouragement to the owners of capital, and entrepreneurial and organisational ability. What about the landless labourer, the small farmer and the working class? They are vital parts of the productive process, but it is seldom that their interests determine incentives. Distributive justice would correct this one-sidedness in the understanding and decisions about incentives. Similarly, we operate with a highly non-egalitarian notion of property. All wealth is created by the co-operation of capital and labour. Property is part of this wealth. But the fight of inheritance vests only in the descendants of one partner in production, namely capital, without recognising the right of the other factor's lineage.

The thrust of these arguments is to show that a high rate of growth which alone can lead to self-reliance is dependent on distributive justice. Today, in all parts of the world, not only in developing countries, there is a revolt of the disinherited. Unless society gives them their due the productive process will be constantly disrupted. Pursuit of policies based on social justice is the only way to overcome the dissatisfaction of the masses and ensure their full support to development programmes.

VI

It needs to be pointed out that this view of social justice as the over-arching goal of development is different from the welfare state approach. The latter is based on enlightened self-interest of owning classes, who under the pressure of class-conflict reluctantly made some concessions to submerged groups, to ensure their own survival and dominant economic and political position. Thus it is essentially a class-doctrine though considerably tamed and civilised by the increasing role played by the State in assuring a more equitable sharing of wealth. The concept of social justice is not based on enlightened self-interest of the dominant groups, but on the basic right of all people to equality and human dignity.

There are other problems in applying the welfare state approach internationally. First of all developing nations are neither sufficiently united nor do they dispose of adequate economic, political and military power to present a threat to the developed; at least not in the near future. So the classic pattern of class-conflict falls down when applied to "North-South" relations. Secondly, the welfare states are them-selves "two-class societies" composed of haves and have-nots on the basis of racial, ethnic and economic factors. To project this approach to the world would mean extending inequality and class difference. Only when social justice imbues policies of welfare states, can it be hoped that the movement to a welfare world will be egalitarian. Not otherwise. Therefore, the "one-world approach" which has shaped much of the ecumenical thinking on development should be built on social justice, nationally and internationally, rather than on enlight-ened self-interest of the dominant group of nations.

VII

From the experience of the sixties it can be concluded that international economic co-operation has not helped in leading developing nations towards self-reliance. I submit that this is so because of a lack of economic justice in international policies dealing with trade, investment and aid.

Aid is considered good if it leads to no aid, i. e. it helps to increase the production and export capacity of recipients to the point where they can finance their development efforts. Foreign loans, which constitute the bulk of aid, would be helpful if they generate a self-liquidating process, i. e., enable the borrower to produce enough to meet internal requirements and have a surplus for repayment of debts. Inflow of foreign technology is creative only if it initiates and sustains a technological revolution in developing nations so that they can progress from imitation to adaptation and thence to innovation. On the whole, the pattern of international economic co-operation has not led to such results.

The burden of debt repayments has increased to the point where nearly half of the current external assistance is used up by developing nations for debt repayments. At this rate by 1980 some developing countries will have to earmark all their aid for repayments, so that the net inflow of external resources will be zero. Prospects of increase in the export earnings of developing nations are not bright. The failure of UNCTAD II highlights these difficulties. Imported technology imposes a two-fold burden on us. First, it is capital-using and labour-saving. Therefore, it generates a demand for resources which are scarce without creating opportunities to absorb abundant resources. Second, in industrial nations it leads to a reduction of imported raw material inputs per unit of output and at the same time increases production of substitutes for some of our vital export commodities. Either way, the exports of developing nations suffer. On the other hand, our growing dependence on imported technology, machinery and industrial raw materials creates an inelasticity of demand as a result of which terms of trade move against developing nations. The burdens imposed by private foreign investment are too well known to be identified here.

Such a pattern of international economic relationships confers greater advantages on developed nations and thus increases existing economic inequalities between rich and poor nations. It is basically non-egalitarian. At UNCTAD II a number of important policy suggestions were accepted in principle but no developed nation seems to be in a hurry to implement them. These related to unilateral preference, transfer of 1 % of GNP as aid to developing countries, stabilising prices of primary commodities, improving terms of loans, etc. It is quite possible that pursuit of such policies may not confer short-term advantages on developed nations. Therefore, enlightened self-interest may not provide the necessary motivation for implementing them. Despite that, if we are pleading for international economic relationships that are more favourable to the weaker group of nations, so that there may be a more just allocation of economic power, we are, in fact, extending the concept of social justice to the international economy. This would be a rational approach once we accept the logic of social justice at the national level.

International economic justice is the only way to ensure development with international interdependence. Otherwise the burdens imposed by existing conditions will gradually force developing nations to a policy of closed development. The choice then is between self-reliance through just international economic policies, and a drift into neo-isolationism, with rich and poor nations closing in on themselves. That would be an anachronism in view of the possibilities offered by the technological revolution. Here is a revolution of possibilities to meet the revolution of rising expectations of the less-developed nations. But so far we have failed to work out a constructive and dynamic relation between possibilities and needs. We should give up harping on enlightened self-interest as the motivating force for new international relations, and substitute social justice in its place. I realise that this will sound idealistic, even utopian. Governments and business interests do not operate on such sentimental bases! Perhaps not even the strategists of ecumenical assistance for development! But if we consider such an approach valid for domestic policies, on economic and political grounds, why not for international policy as well? This may be one situation where what is sauce for the national geese is also sauce for the international gander!

VIII

To attain the goal of social justice, it becomes necessary to change the social framework. For example, within a nation it would mean a change in existing property relations, position of social classes, land tenure system, etc. It would be wrong to assume that policies of welfare and distributive justice would of themselves establish new social relations. On the contrary it is only by changing existing relations that a nation is enabled to pursue policies of social justice. In other words, a radical restructuring of society is an essential prerequisite for achieving social justice. That is why this approach is structuralist.

"Lack of political will" has been identified as the main obstacle to more egalitarian international economic policies. But it is the existing social framework which is responsible for this lack. Thistles do not produce grapes, even with modern technology! When social justice becomes the dominant concern of national policies it will change domestic social framework which would then eliminate the lack of political will that has obstructed egalitarian international policies.

Change in the social framework calls for a political approach to economic and social issues. The kind of neutral economic approach inherent in popular development theories and models ignores the significance of structural change. It assumes, in the *laissez-faire* vein, that resources will bring about economic growth, and that will improve relations between groups and classes. So we take political and structural factors as given and are concerned only with the use of resources for optimum production. But resources will give the right results only when the right conditions are provided for them. Experience of developing nations is showing that these are structural rather than technical conditions.

In some cases a high rate of growth can be obtained without major structural changes. But that would enhance the power of entrenched dominant groups which resist change for social justice. As a result there develops a chronic instability in the political situation which not only negates earlier gains, but makes further efforts for rapid economic growth abortive. Therefore, if we really think that political will is a vital determinant of economic policies, we are recognising the importance, indeed the primacy of changes in the social framework.

Such politicization of economic perspective raises the issue of pragmatism and ideology. By and large, ecumenical thinking leans towards pragmatism. Much depends on what we mean by the term. If it means trying to act as effectively as we can in a given situation, it is a realistic and partly valid viewpoint. But our concern for human needs and development of societies should take us a step further. We are trying to act in a given situation in order to change the situation. For it is the given situation that is responsible for the maladies we are trying to cure. If we interpret pragmatism to mean a neutrality to the situation that prevails, we are trying to solve a problem without dealing with the structural factors that cause it.

However, if pragmatism also implies changing the situation, then it takes on a dynamic form. There can be changes that are regressive and changes that are progressive. Obviously, we are not for *any* change but for change that is progressive. That means we operate with some ideology. There is bound to be a debate about what kind of ideology, and so on. That is natural; in fact, necessary. One man's ideological meat may be another man's poison. But there is no escaping ideology, as we sometimes try to. To say that we wish to follow a pragmatic rather than an ideological approach is a contradiction in terms. That kind of pragmatism accepts existing conditions and, therefore, becomes an ideology of the status-quo. Repeated affirmations of pragmatism do not make one any less ideological. The question is are we pragmatists who support the ideology of the *status quo*, or pragmatists who support the ideology of radical change? Let us all be pragmatists if that is ecumenically more respectable. I for one, will have no quarrel with that. But let us stand up and be counted: for change or for stagnation.

This would be the right place to say a few words about development and revolution. It is believed, and rightly, that development will lead to stability and conditions of lasting peace. But many have distorted this idea and interpreted it to mean that only stability can ensure development. By stability they mean an undisturbed continuance of present political, economic and social structures. But it is precisely this kind of stability that is change-resisting, hence, development-denying. Development cannot take place without radical changes in economic and social relationships, and diffusion of political power. Such changes are accompanied by instability, disorder, upheaval. We completely misunderstand the process of development if we equate it with static stability.

Thus understood, development is revolution. Revolution means a radical change in the values and structures of society. It is neither a state of perennial anarchy nor necessarily a call to violence. Non-violent revolution is a new phenomenon in human history and I believe that it represents the wave of the future. The objective of revolution is to acquire power in order to establish institutions and policies that will lead to certain social goals. The anti-institutional kind of revolution is as self-contradictory as the stability kind of development. If revolution is for gaining power and using power how can it operate without organisation and institutions? One can be against this or that kind of "establishment", but one has to be for some kind of "establishment". A purely anti-institutional view of revolution is laissez-fairist and reactionary. It assumes that tearing down existing structures will of itself bring about progress. How is this different from the classical idea of the "invisible hand"?

A revolutionary approach has to be a structuralist approach, i. e., first tearing down then building up. It is true that one cannot make an omelette without breaking eggs. But it is equally true that one can break an egg and not necessarily have an omelette. Some other ingredients and a minimum of culinary skill are necessary for converting the raw egg into a more delicious dish. Revolution is goal-directed; it is not an end in itself. And development is both an adjunct of and a goal of revolution. May I therefore submit that where a development *versus* revolution debate is carried on it is due to a misunderstanding of both. The two should be seen as mutually sustaining. Together they lead society from static stability to creative instability.

IX

Having indicated the framework in which development projects should be fitted, I would like to make some suggestions about projects for which ecumencal assistance may be given. My assumption is that the bulk, if not the whole, of such assistance would go to non-governmental projects, mainly, though not necessarily, church-related. Perhaps some resources could go to government-sponsored projects as well. Personally I would question the direct use of ecumenical resources for governmental projects. If we wish to co-operate in financing any such project, the best way would be through multilaterally assisted UN specialised agencies. And now for some observations: One, development projects should contribute to the goals of development. That is self-evident, but it should be both an objective and a criterion. A project is valid if it promotes social justice and in the process strengthens forces of self-reliance, and thus accelerates the rate of growth. We have to see development projects as catalysts and change-generators, otherwise they have no justification. Difficulties could occur where the government in power is change-resisting. Generally non-governmental projects are expected to adhere to overall government policy. But if that policy is *status quo* oriented, a project geared to it ceases to be a development project. Two options exist. Either close it down because it cannot fulfil its objectives. That is the easy way out. Or continue despite official frowns. If tensions reach the point where it is impossible to pull on, the project would at least have sown the seeds of discontent that will one day bring about change. Tactfulness and diplomacy are essential for co-ordinating non-governmental projects with national development programme. But our basic loyalty is to development and its goals. If official policy obstructs or subverts these, then tactfulness to assure continuance would tantamount to betrayal. For it is not the continuance of ecumenical projects or the satisfaction we have by being engaged in developmental work that is important, but the movement towards development.

Two, non-governmental projects can have a place so long as a nation pursues policies which allow voluntary agencies a role in national development. Chances are that many governments in developing countries will follow such policies. But the same may not hold for inflow of private resources from outside. These could be stopped either permanently or during particular periods of crisis. We must take note of such a possibility in deciding the pattern of ecumenical assistance. Should national development funds be set up as parts of an international ecumenical fund so as to assure finances for projects even if resources from outside are blocked?

Three, there is the vital question of financial self-reliance of development projects as such. Most church-related projects in developing countries have so far been totally or largely dependent on funds from churches and ecumenical agencies in developed nations. This pattern of dependence has continued for a very, very long time. It differs fundamentally from the pattern of foreign assistance to nations. This needs to be appreciated by Christian friends who say that if governments are getting resources from outside what is wrong if churches and Christian agencies do the same? In the case of governments two points have to be recognised. First, that foreign assistance constitutes a small part, generally less than 15 %, of the total resources used for development. The overwhelming share of developmental resources is national. Second, the stated policy is to use foreign assistance for self-reliance, not for continued dependence. Only if we can fulfil these two conditions in church-related programmes dependent on external resources, would we be justified in comparing our situation to that of governments.

Therefore, it is of the first importance to examine this question and devise ways and means of making recipient Christian agencies self-reliant. Should ecumenical assistance take on a double function from the outset: one, to provide necessary resources to a project, and two, to provide substantial funds to national Christian agencies to build income-raising projects that would promote self-reliance?

Four, what should be the agency through which development projects are established and run? Under the new style of ecumenical operations the tendency is to set up a new organization for each important new project. There are many advantages in this. But I would suggest that established Christian institutions — educational, medical, welfare, etc., of which there are many in developing countries, be considered for taking up responsibility for development projects. I adduce five arguments in support of this viewpoint:

(i) Such institutions are already known and accepted by the total community, hence it would be easier to get community support and participation for new programmes initiated by them.

(ii) Some development projects are by nature short-term and temporary. There are better chances of that happening if they are linked with institutions which have continuity than if set up autonomously. In the latter case a project develops a vested interest in its continuation, as has been the experience of a number of so-called "temporary" ecumenical projects. To obviate this danger of institutionalism it would be prudent to make development projects as extension programmes of existing institutions.

(iii) Quite a few well-established institutions may be better equipped in terms of leadership, organisational efficiency, sense of stewardship, ability to associate people with programmes, and so on. A lack of some of these qualities has often been the major bottleneck in many ecumenical projects.

(iv) If I can generalise from the experience of India, Christian institutions are credited by the general public with pioneering qualities. This may be more a reference to a past virtue which no longer characterises our work. But the public image of such institutions is also a measure of public expectation from them. Today, when new ground has to be broken in the area of social action, a linking up of development projects with existing institutions may enable them to recapture their pioneering heritage. If that happens it could counteract and even overcome the creeping paralysis of institutionalism that plagues old units. I can see the danger that existing deficiencies in institutions could contaminate young and dynamic projects. On the other hand, the dynamism and potential creativity of new projects may save the soul of the old. It is a risk worth taking.

(v) Educational institutions can become agencies for training of leadership and creating attitudes favourable to change. Perhaps the existing pattern of education and the general functioning of educational institutions has failed to play such a role. But development-biased extension programmes could make up the prevailing deficiencies. A direct interaction between motivation-building projects and the moribund educational pattern may be the catalyst that speeds up change in this vital sector of national life. Whatever be the limitations of these institutions, the fact is that they shape ideas and attitudes of those to whom leadership eventually comes.

Five, an important task of development projects is to help the process of self-reliance. This calls for research to evolve techniques with greater indigenous-orientation, as will utilise resources available in the country, and unearth and create new resources. Very little has been done in this area so far, certainly not in ecumenically assisted projects. We hear and talk about intermediate technology but continue to get enmeshed in advanced technology which is received ready-made from developed nations. A movement from imitation to innovation is an essential part of the thrust towards self-reliance.

Equally important is self-reliance in ideas. We need to make organised efforts through projects to promote authentic social thought in developing countries, based upon the ethos of that society and geared to its problems and potentialities.

Six, it is also important to establish some projects on a regional basis. This would allow increased intra-regional co-operation and enable developing nations to benefit from each others' experience. Obviously they have more in common with each other than with developed nations. In fact, leadership training programmes should be region-based. While there are benefits in training and experience gained in developed nations, that tends to generate a western approach to problems which are very different, and may to some extent be responsible for the frustrations that lead to brain drain.

Seven, it is important to discover practical ways in which the style of operation of ecumenically assisted projects can reflect social justice. If it is patterned on the same kind of economic differentials between foreign and national and between different categories of nationals as exists in projects run by governments and private companies, it will miss a great opportunity to demonstrate what we believe should be a new style of functioning. This is a complicated problem but we must wrestle with it in order to play a pioneering role in this area.

These suggestions and questions leave out more than they include, and should be taken as indicative rather than exhaustive. The basic question is how to incorporate the approach which we may agree upon, in the actual formulation, financing and implementation of projects? How do we make projects subserve the larger goals of development?

Theorising on development has usefulness only if it can be increasingly concretised in projects and programmes. Otherwise it is an arid intellectual exercise which we in ecumenical circles would do well to avoid in the context of the pressing needs of society today.

Development Projects and Concern for Structural Changes

by Helder P. Camara

I. Indispensable initial considerations

You have the joy of being men of faith, Christians. It is therefore important that I should tell you that this message of mine is the outcome of prayer and personal intercession. Just because it sums up a great deal of my own experience as a shepherd in the Church in the North-East of Brazil (one of the most discussed and most traumatised places in the world), I asked Christ *not* to let me transmit a view which is too impassioned and too personal.

There are far more than two or three of us gathered here in His name; the Master is therefore here in our midst. In every thought and word I shall bear in mind that He is present with us, listening to us, and that He will judge the statements that we make and the proposals that we submit.

How can I thank our Father for this atmosphere of faith, which will enable me to speak to you as if I were standing before the supreme judge, and rendering account to Him of my thoughts, words, actions and omissions, when speaking to you about "Development Projects and Concern for Structural Changes"?

II. The situation is a unique opportunity presented to Christians by God, our Father

1. *The sad reality, the marvellous prospects, the possibility (even the probability) of a tragic conclusion.*

The present situation of mankind may be described briefly and objectively as follows: a sad reality, marvellous prospects, the possibility (even the probability) of a tragic conclusion.

It is a sad fact that, according to the statement of the Beirut Conference (1968), 80 % of the world's resources are at the disposal of

20 % of the world's inhabitants, "while one segment of humanity is rich and growing richer, the rest will struggle in varying degrees of poverty and have little certainty of breaking out of their stagnation in the next decades".

The prospects are marvellous because, as we all know, for the first time in history, man is in the position to fulfil the command of the Creator to dominate Nature and to complete His work of creation. For the first time the technological resources available would enable us "to promote the good of every man and of the whole man".

The conclusion may be (and probably will be) tragic, owing to the blindness of the privileged 20 % of mankind who think it "normal" to spend 150 billion dollars per annum on armaments, but can hardly scrape together 10 billion for economic and social cooperation (to quote again from the Beirut Report).

2. *A unique opportunity for Christians*

Our responsibility as Christians makes us tremble. The Northern hemisphere, the developed area of the world, the 20 % who possess 80 % of the world's resources, are of Christian origin. What impression can our African and Asian brethren and the masses in Latin America have of Christianity, if the tree is to be judged by its fruits? For we Christians are largely responsible for the unjust world in which we live.

Christianity is invoked in order to lead a sort of crusade against Communism. Christianity is invoked in order to combat the wave of hatred, deep-rooted resentment and terror which is rising everywhere.

The 20 % who let 80 % stagnate in a situation which is often sub-human — what right have they to allege that Communism crushes the human person? The 20 % who are keeping 80 % in a situation which is often sub-human — are they or are they not responsible for the violence and hatred which are beginning to break out all over the world?

During the course of centuries the injustices have become more and more firmly entrenched, and have perpetuated themselves to such an extent that we have come to accept them as the "social order" which should be defended and safeguarded. While all this was going on, we

Christians have detached ourselves from the problems of this world so much that we have made it easier for injustice to take root.

Even sadder than this is the spectacle presented by us, Christians, torn by our struggles and dissensions which destroy the seamless robe of Christ.

In spite of this, it is easier for Christians of different denominations to cooperate in an effort to assist man (which is one of the commandments laid upon us by the Gospel) than it is to unite around the Eucharistic table, or even to unite in hearing the word of God.

What a splendid testimony we could give if we were to unite with our Christian brethren in the developed countries to do everything in our power to overcome the egoism of the Northern hemisphere — which is the Christian hemisphere, or at any rate Christian in origin! If we were to do our utmost to influence the Northern hemisphere to re-examine the implications of justice in its relations with the under-developed countries!

What a splendid testimony we could give to our non-Christian brethren in Africa and Asia, and to the masses in Latin America (who are more easily moved by feeling than by personal conviction) if we were to unite, so as to try to carry out the fine convictions expressed in the reports from Medellin, Uppsala and Beirut!

3. *We have enough theory to work on for the moment*

I have referred to the conclusions reached at Medellin (Meeting of the Catholic Hierarchy of Latin America), at Uppsala (IVth Assembly of the World Council of Churches) and at Beirut (Conference on World Cooperation for Development organised by the World Council of Churches and the Pontifical Commission Justice and Peace). If we add the Encyclical Populorum Progressio of Pope Paul VI we can say that for the next few years we Christians do not require any more documents concerning the social sphere. The problem that we now have to tackle is that of putting our fine theories into practice.

This is where the difficulties arise, both externally and internally. Usually the privileged 20 % and the governments welcome effusively documents like those mentioned above, and say that they are in complete agreement with them. But as soon as someone decides to apply these documents (to which so much tribute is paid) he is immediately accused of being subversive and of being a Communist.

Everyone agrees that abuses and wrongs exist in the socio-economic and politico-cultural structures. But (say the governments and the privileged section) it is impossible in a few days, a few months or even a few years to change things which have taken centuries to build up. Many Christian leaders are deterred by the fear that if changes are too rapid they may upset the "social order", undermine the principle of authority and destroy private ownership.

It is then that division starts within the Church itself, disagreement between the cautious, moderate people who want quiet, gradual, unhurried change and those who feel that there is no time to be lost because we have already to catch up on centuries of stagnation, and have to confess serious sins of omission. The *social order?* But what social order are they talking about? The one that we see today, which consists in leaving millions of God's children in miserable poverty, should rather be called *social disorder*, systematized injustice. *Private ownership?* Is it not evident to everyone that on this point we Christians have abandoned the Fathers of the Church, and that we have ended by attributing divine right to private ownership, whereas God's law says that the wealth of the world should be shared by all, and should never form odious, oppressive monopolies?

One allegation also made by the privileged section and by the government is that the documents issued by the Church demanding structural changes are extremely vague. They say what is wrong, but they lose themselves in generalisations instead of indicating concrete solutions. This objection alarms some Christians, because they fear that denouncing what is wrong and urging structural changes without giving concrete indications for action, is preparing the way for agitators and Communists.

4.   Anti-Communism, what follies are committed in thy name!

You have certainly noticed what follies and cruelties are committed on the pretext of preventing subversion and combatting Communism.

The first consequence is that the existing structures are maintained — structures in which centuries of violence are entrenched, for they protect the privileges of a minority at the expense of the poverty of millions. Then totalitarian methods are adopted, informers are encouraged; everyone suspects everyone else; liberty is completely suspended, including freedom of speech; the atmosphere is one of complete insecurity, arbitrary imprisonment, moral and physical torture employed in order to extort confessions. Do not think that I am alluding to any particular country; the serious thing is that the anti-Communist obsession leads logically to these methods which, in turn, lead to ever-increasing antagonism and violence.

Anyone who is sincerely democratic, who believes in the power of truth and love and wants to speak, is unable to do so, for he is unable to write or to hold meetings. His intentions are misinterpreted and he has no opportunity to state the truth. It is impossible to believe what the political prisoners say or what they have said. Surely it is easy to understand why young people, especially, resort to clandestine action and try to combat violence with violence?

At this point it is possible to envisage the rôle (perhaps a decisive one) which the World Council of Churches and the Pontifical Comission Justice and Peace are called to play in God's plans, as the concience of the really free world, and as the mouthpiece of those who cannot speak for themselves.

5. *Points to be clearly kept in view*

In order that you should be able to understand the concrete proposition which I am putting before you, there are certain points which should be clearly kept in view.

It is not by chance that we, as Christians, are so closely concerned with the problem of the distance, which becomes daily more striking, between the developed and underdeveloped world. Let us have the humility and the courage to acknowledge that we are, to a large extent, responsible for allowing injustice between men to have reached so far, since this injustice stems from the hemisphere which, at least in origin, is Christian. In actual fact we have to atone for our sins of omission.

Injustice is the right word to use. In the developed countries, when one is thinking about the poorer countries, the temptation is to imagine that basically the problem is a racial one (there are the whites and then ... the others — black, yellow and mulatto — in the rest of the world), a racial problem aggravated by a certain unwillingness to come to terms with it, by dishonesty, and above all, recently, by the demographic explosion. We could debate these views and prejudices one by one. However, even if they were valid, this should not be a pretext for forgetting that there exist places in the world where decisions are made, imperial capitals where international policies are drawn up, where prices are fixed, where measures are taken whereby the rich countries always become more rich or the poorer countries always more poor.

It is easy and convenient for the rich countries, when face to face with the poorer countries, to think in terms of financial and technical aid, the result being, nearly always, that the aid is just apparent and leads to the actual despoiling of the poorer countries. It is inconvenient for the rich countries to work out effective changes in the socio-economic, political or cultural structures of the poor countries, for the very simple reason that they would no longer need to provide the raw materials essential for the administration and expansion of the developing economies.

We should not delude ourselves: a change in structure of the underdeveloped countries would not be possible without a change in structure of the developed countries. The expression must be taken literally. It is not merely concerned with a change in mentality with regard to the poor countries: it concerns a profound change in international commercial policy. How much longer are we going to permit international trusts to make small groups of men fabulously wealthy, while they keep millions of others in slavery? I do not want to be told that every day trusts are becoming more democratic because millions and millions of ordinary people are becoming share-holders and thus have a control over the concern ... Share-holders, yes, in the sense that they hold a few meagre shares, but without any say in the management of the trust, which is carried out anonymously, impassively and coldly by a group of people who do not mind coming face to face with those they have crushed.

It is no use asserting that there are laws which control the investment of profits abroad. Who does not know that there are numerous ways of evading these laws?

It is not honest to say that the rich countries invest in the poor countries purely out of generosity and the desire to help as they have sufficient internal markets and no longer need raw materials now that there are so many substitutes.

6. Aid, perhaps decisive, in changing unjust and oppressive structures

The World Council of Churches, and the Pontifical Commission Justice and Peace, could set the example, during the present period of violence and deeply entrenched attitudes, of using the non-violent action of the peacemakers to good effect by creating a movement of public opinion, on the European scale, which would perhaps bring moral pressure to bear, leading to a change in structure here as a prior condition to bringing about a change in structure of the underdeveloped countries.

Just imagine that the World Council and the Pontifical Commission were to arrange for a basic document to be drawn up by experts, summarizing the principal points of the Reports of the first three Conferences of the United Nations Conference on Trade and Development.

We all know that the three Conferences of UNCTAD — two of which took place in Geneva — constitute the most important steps taken by the underdeveloped world to bring about a recognition of its rights with regard to the developed world. And we also all know how the USA and the USSR, typical representatives of capitalist and socialist countries, both showed an equal lack of sensibility and comprehension when confronted by countries concerned with rising out of their misery.

This basic document summarizing the UNCTAD Reports should be sent by the World Council and the Pontifical Commission to the principal European universities on both sides of the Iron Curtain, inviting them to a Seminar, at which would be decided once and for all, whether, on the world scale, relations between countries of plenty and countries of poverty are just or unjust.

A meeting of experts from the principal European universities would cause a stir and attract the press, both written and spoken, of the whole continent. The World Council and the Pontifical Commission would be prepared to:

— point out that the press in the developed countries has already bypassed the stage at which, on the whole, it only described the folklore of the countries of the Third World: today it has made the world realize that famine, poverty and underdevelopment do in fact exist;

— supply details enabling one to follow more closely the university debate on the essential relationships between development and underdeveloped countries.

The World Council and the Pontifical Commission would profit by inviting key-persons of the main religions of the world. As all religions have a direct and vital interest in world peace, they would be shown to what extent peace is compromised by injustices on a world-wide scale. All the religions would be asked to unite and to bring all the moral forces they possess to an achievement of justice, prime-condition for peace.

Other meetings, which it is hoped could be arranged, towards this movement of public opinion, which, from Europe, would extend throughout the world, would be:

— a meeting of the leaders of all the main political parties of Europe;

— a meeting of the heads of business-concerns and leaders of trade-unions, with effective repercussions in their respective classes;

— a meeting of experts in techniques and structures, the probable technocrats of tomorrow.

III. How should we break down the walls of Jericho?

Far be it for us to forget that God exists and that He has and always will have the right of interfering in the natural order.

We bear witness to the fact that our Creator and Father wished us to be formed in His image and likeness and charged us to hold sway over nature and complete the creation.

When you ask if it is possible to quote the example of a country which, without armed violence, has been able to change its structures, it is possible to reply that up until very recently, humanity did not possess the powerful means of social communication which we have today.

However, it so happens that in underdeveloped countries, those who wish to upset the existing structures, even if they use democratic methods, lose access to these powerful means of social communication, even if, at the same time, they do not lose their civil rights.

Render this service in the cause of peace: without measuring the sacrifices, try to prove that truth, love and faith, with the divine blessing, are capable of moving and breaking down the walls of Jericho.

Development Projects and Concern for Structural Changes

by Erhard Eppler

I. Structural changes — a criterion for successful development policy

There is no need for me to explain to this audience that structural changes are necessary, that they are even a prerequisite for development in every sense of the world. The misery of a large part of mankind is not the result simply of a lack of food, capital, know-how, technical equipment or of certain human qualities such as initiative, enterprise and organizational skill. Underdevelopment is primarily due to the inadequacy of the social structures in the countries concerned, as well as in the industrialized countries and in international society.

It is still a wide-spread practice today to describe the situation in the distressed areas of the world in terms of quantitative data, giving figures on income and literacy, and the number of hospital beds per unit of population. However, we know that figures convey a false picture unless they are supplemented by an analysis of power relationships, dependencies, vested privileges, rigid institutions and systems which keep producing similar, unfair conditions no matter how large the quantity of aid may be in terms of capital and technical know-how.

Statistics of economic success sometimes hide the fact that it is only the wealth of a small class or of foreign companies that is increasing. A country's oil revenue may produce a high per capita income in the statistical records, but often enough be of no benefit to the people in the slum areas.

On the other hand, the fact remains that talking about development without paying attention to the laws of economics is of no use. The revival of political economics in contemporary studies and research shows that economic action must take the cultural, social and, above all, political conditions and repercussions into account, and that objectives of a social nature must be given priority.

The objective

Our difficulties begin when it comes to determining the structural changes that are wanted, and the price that can and may be actually paid for this.

An easy way to put it would be as follows: The objective of structural changes must be to remove all obstacles that hinder self-sustained economic growth, prevent the fair distribution of the goods available and keep people from taking a reasonable share in decisions concerning their own affairs. No one will contradict this. Theoretical consensus may also be reached if the problem to be solved concerns villages in the bush, the slums in the cities, young orphans and the disabled. The critical stage is reached as soon as politics become involved, that is, when the existing balance of power, distribution of wealth and status in a society is affected. Changes in national or regional societies bear upon international interests. In some cases, changes in the structure of society cannot be initiated successfully unless changes in the international structure of power and economic relationships are made. In our world, where everything is becoming more and more interrelated, it is still possible to launch individual projects designed to change the social structure locally, but in making any structural changes, national balance and the international balance of power must be kept in mind. This involves both special obligations and opportunities for the Churches which are communicating with human society at all levels, while at the same time they can afford to take a detached view.

In discussing our objective, we must further realize that we are bound to act under time pressure. We cannot let new institutions and behaviours gradually "grow" as we used to in former times. Rising birth rates, rapid urbanization and rising expectations are putting pressure on us. Mankind cannot wait; it must often enforce changes.

II. Multiple changes, not simply revolution

These preliminary thoughts may seem to vindicate those who call for a worldwide simultaneous revolution, that is, for a strategy of everything or nothing, to obtain the complete and instantaneous change of all existing societies. In fact, I think it is true that the winds of change we feel blowing across our earth today will spare no section of any society in the long run.

In different societies, different kinds of changes are necessary. It is not enough to refer to capitalism and industrialized countries as the key to all evils in the world.

It may be that in some societies, socialist-motivated liberation movements aiming at centrally-controlled states with planned social and economic development will give quite useful indications as to what changes are needed. On the other hand, there is no reason to follow these particular bearings towards all the necessary social changes in the world. There are states in which it is really the established forces who deserve our support in their efforts to form (out of tribes scattered over a vast territory) something like a viable nation, able to compete in the international field. Think, for example, of Tanzania. Here the term "revolution" has an entirely different meaning from what is usual in some Latin American societies. There simply cannot be a dogmatic, uniform prescription for all. We cannot describe the objectives of social change by means of terms and pictures from the text-books of western and eastern ideologies.

We must remain open. Remaining open also means cooperating with states whose systems are somewhat dubious, if this can help to drive development one step forward. A sound tax system, land reform, stripping parasitic classes of their power, may promote development also if action along these lines were initiated in the first place for nationalistic reasons. Also here, the motives are less decisive than the actual effects. The latter certainly also include the price of human suffering, new injustice, of the destruction of cultural values which must be paid.

III. The possible price of upheavals

Anyone who wants to create two, three or many Vietnams all over the world today must be prepared to reckon with not only the Third World War, i. e. the great worldwide showdown of the super-powers and super-weapons, but also with an isolationist, perhaps even fascist reaction from the industrialized societies. Left-wing theorists have often prophesied that what they call latent fascism in the industrialized societies will become a manifest fascist defence reaction to the liberation movements in the Third World. This is, so to speak, included and accepted as the price of revolution.

Development policy is the art of promoting changes in a pragmatic way without endangering the small degree of order, regulated communication among the states, economies and societies, and humanity that is still left after the era of colonialism and world wars. The wholesale condemnation of systems as such is a blind and tactically stupid policy.

IV. Strategical considerations

We must, therefore, start off in a flexible, pluralistic, perhaps even contradictory manner, e. g., appeal to the common sense in the ruling forces, say, in the younger management groups while at the same time encouraging and promoting reformist groups and remaining in contact with the revolutionary elements. What is decisive is the opportunity of actually making structures more dynamic.

V. Project policy

Which projects then have a real chance of succes in these conditions?

I believe that a peaceful change of structures is possible. However, we do not place our hopes only on the contradictions of the established interest groups and on the limits with which the expansion of even the most powerful economic and military forces are faced today, but much more on what has been called the chance of the "fruitful misunderstanding".

Let me give an example. A feudal ruler who regards his land and subjects practically as family property becomes rich and gains more power as a result of the exploitation of an oilwell by a foreign company — the classic case of "vertical" imperialism. But what will he do with the money under present-day conditions? He will perhaps live expensively, but probably he will also build schools — not, of course, in order that the children should be educated there to critical thinking, but in order to train better subjects. But what is the objective result of such efforts? There will be growing numbers of school children and students in that country. More communication will be possible. Objectively speaking, social conditions have at least been set for the next step.

The question is, however, whether such effects can be planned. Changes in social structures do not automatically develop in the direction desired. One could quote a long list of examples which would show that the social consequences of large-scale economic and technical projects aggravated rather than improved the previous situation. There are certainly "unfruitful misunderstandings" as well as "fruitful" ones.

Take, for example, the people who were brought out of the bush to work on the expansion of a large aluminium works, which afterwards could employ only a few specialists after its completion. Thousands did not return to the bush. Instead, estranged from their original way of life, they moved into the nearest large towns and increased the numbers of the proletariat there.

Coordinated strategy

Here is an important task for Church planners. It must be possible to induce the big international financial institutions like the World Bank to include in future sociological considerations in their projects during the early planning stage. Sociologists, ethnologists, educational planners and social workers ought to be consulted during the preliminary examination of a project every bit as much as economists and banking experts. The World Bank is also in a position to ensure that the social consequences of these programmes are kept under control by implementing concomitant measures. I have been told that the first step towards such cooperation with Church authorities has been made.

Criteria for designing special schemes to improve on the social structure

Integration with major projects involving technical assistance and capital aid has one consequence which smaller measures of social and educational assistance do not necessarily produce, i. e. an immediately noticeable impact on everyone concerned. It is, as it were, a forcible process of adaptation. This brings us to the prerequisites of any successful design for change in the social structure of a community.

a)   The first step is to produce the initial impulse. This may also come from a natural disaster, from Government programmes or political changes. In many African states, the initial impulse was provided by the liberation from colonial rule: this lent wings to people's expectations and led to a certain willingness to accept innovations.

b)   However, the main need is finding a partner who will take charge of the project and accept responsibility for it. In the case of projects which are designed to change the structure of society, active minorities (groups who are prepared to take the initiative) will have to be asked to come forward and be enabled to translate their own ideas into reality. The external form of a project or its technical and economic circumstances then are of secondly importance. The paramount consideration here is man, not the project. By way of contrast, most schemes of technical assistance and capital aid are based on factural considerations. First, the plan is drawn up in the light of technical and other factors; the necessary funds are set aside and the economic preconditions fulfilled; and finally skilled staff and advisers are engaged. The project comes first, then the personnel.

The problem of finding partners sometimes leads to conflicts: even progressive forces often are not agreed among themselves. There is a risk of finding oneself involuntarily taking sides in a dispute because of the assistance one has granted. Yet such disputes can only be solved on the spot by local people. Various cadres will claim to be the true spokesman for the underprivileged. Which groups are really entitled to speak up and on whose behalf? The situation is simple if the group behind the scheme is an official institution of the country in question; but it becomes difficult if it is in opposition to the authorities in power. One solution is to make a pluralistic approach and promote several of the relevant groups at the same time. Moreover, new responsible institutions may have to be created if the available partners are not suitable or if, in the course of time, they get into a position which renders useful work difficult.

More than one Christian community, for example, is said to have become alienated from its own environment or even its neighbouring community as a result of contacts with Church aid agencies in industrial countries, rather than induced to work in a Christian spirit for the well-being also of their non-Christian neighbourhood. Anybody who has access to development aid funds may easily become a privileged person without wishing to do so.

Anyone who administers development aid funds takes over responsibility for selecting effective partners. A formal title such as being the community "locally concerned" is insufficient — as indeed is good will. What we need are objective criteria; willingness to make a contribution of one's own; judicious planning; a guarantee that once the initiative has been taken, it will be continued; and finally contacts with one's environment and the general population. Then again, there must be a willingness to work with others and to account for one's actions.

Also making compromises cannot be ruled out, and sometimes help has to be furnished in cases where there are few indications of any self-help. We cannot limit ourselves to a cool computation of profitability or make action dependent on whether success is likely or not. In this respect, we are worlds apart from many economists and Marxists, who are quite ready to sacrifice the human element for the operational success of a project. Let me quote an example from Government development aid. When certain local authorities in North Brazil approached us with a request for help, there was no lack of people who advised us not to invest any money there. The chances of success in South Brazil were much better, they said. If the North East was to be given effective assistance, vast sums of money would be required. And if we decided to provide aid, we should not do so in the poorest districts, but in the coastal areas so as to slowly move the frontier of development in to the interior of the country. In spite of all this, we do support programmes even in the poorest areas of the North East. Why? Because some groups there pursued activities which seemed to deserve support, and because you simply cannot advise everyone to emigrate to the South. Also those who stay have a claim like anybody else to experience at least some kind of progress.

In other words, the Church must often go out to where man lives in misery and not stop once the area of maximum profitability is left behind. Nevertheless, she ought to use the largest part of her funds where the chances of success are at their best. Success can be expected only if disciplined cadres, anxious to promote development, are available. Projects designed to teach and encourage the right attitudes and to train and guide leaders and managers should be given top priority.

Training must start with the responsible local Church leaders themselves; it should not be directed at individuals but at groups and cadres expected to take charge of projects.

It must also be mentioned, in connection with the promotion of the cadres, that one must be prepared to pay leadership personnel adequate rates of remuneration — in some cases for a fairly long period of time. Many of the Church's development schemes remain an extraneous element in the society in question because they depend on the abilities of foreign staff. Better to win expensive local skill than employ foreign personnel for too long.

c) The main thing is that the message gets through to the masses and that self-help is mobilised. The basic principle of guerilla warfare that the partisans must be supported or at least tolerated by part of the population in order to be able to exist within the society like a fish in the ocean is equally true of the promoters of development aid. There are numerous projects which benefit only a small circle of persons and have no impact on the pattern of society.

An impact restricted to Christian communities and Christian minorities is not sufficient. But if a wider range of people is to be reached, they must also be included in the planning.

Christian communities, by taking charge of projects, are merely first contacts and partners. Later, they should serve as intermediaries, helping to establish contacts with others. Non-Christians ought to participate in the Church's central promotion institutions and regional offices and bear some of the responsibility for the projects. Participation does not mean that the projects should be turned over to them: it implies clear-cut agreements on the scope and aims of cooperation and on the influence they may take. In cases where this can be achieved, even cooperation with groups that take a critical attitude towards the churches ought not to be excluded. What matters is the chance of success for a project.

d) Important for the success of projects which aim at changing the social structure is adequate protection by external groups for a sufficiently long period of time. By "external groups" we mean any authorities or agencies who are not in any way connected with the various local interest groups. Wherever the Government itself is pursuing a systematic plan for bringing about the necessary changes in the social structure the various projects ought to be integrated into the national development plan somewhat in the way it has been done in Tanzania.

e)   The consequences of projects, particularly those meant to improve the social structure, cannot always be calculated in advance. Heightening man's consciousness always means increasing his expectations. People who have learnt to read and write will want books. Anyone who has passed a course of training looks for a suitable job. A co-operative which has learnt to successfully apply modern production methods naturally expects to be able to sell its crops. Projects which have started modestly will reach the stage where they need more capital. There can be no standstill. Larger storage facilities are needed. Then again, a better income makes people more ambitious about schooling for their children. Many projects have failed because the expectations they generated were disappointing. The churches, too, must consider what they can do to keep successful projects going. I am thinking of participation in regional development banks that grant credit without collateral to skilled craftsmen who wish to establish their own workshop. I am thinking of easy-term credits to institutions for self-help in the slums and in the rural areas which are expanding successfully, but need economic and financial support.

The consequence of such an attitude may be that fewer projects are launched. However, those which get under way can be looked after for an extended period of time — at least for long enough for them to make their way and no longer need external assistance.

The opportunities for the churches

The churches and the church-sponsored aid agencies have opportunities which governments and even international organizations do not have. They come into contact with categories of persons who will hardly benefit directly from state or international aid. However, also church-run projects are dependent on the tolerance of the government concerned and they need the protection of international organizations. Hence, it is useful for the churches to cooperate closely with the international institutions. We know from our experience of bilateral official aid that a partner government is often quite ready to accept a loan to

78

build a dam, but would reject any reference to possible social consequences and therefore necessary subsidiary measures as an interference in its internal affairs. Non-state bodies, i. e., including church agencies, sometimes have a better chance to act without offending government susceptibilities. They are not bound by the state system and by the principle of non-interference in internal affairs in the strict sense of the word. Even though they have to show consideration for the churches in the region in question, they are able to cooperate discreetly with other social forces, local associations and institutions within the country without getting involved in the delicacies of official foreign relations.

The churches have both the funds and the moral and political weight to engage, by setting up an independent, international study centre, the services of the best brains in the world on the same scale as, for example, the World Bank does. I imagine that such a centre could tackle precisely those questions pertaining to a change of social structures which even international organizations — dependent as they are on their member governments — often may not mention at all or refer to only in polite and vague terms.

What we need is more exemplary and matter-of-fact studies on the possibilities and obstacles involved in social change, and fewer round-the-board criticisms of the various systems. Such investigation can only be carried out by agencies which have a reputation for objective work and for not being primarily bent on getting their preconceived notions confirmed. Experts working on such studies at the international study centre as suggested above could stand back and take a hard, objective and thorough look at the development policies of national governments and international organizations and judge them above all in the light of clear social standards. The World Bank has engaged a number of first-class banking experts and economists. What the churches could do to match this in the social sphere would be to employ a similarly-qualified staff of experts on social strategy, a kind of socio-cultural consulting agency for advice on projects. At the same time, the performance of developing countries in adapting their social structures to the requirements of modernisation ought to be reviewed and evaluated.

A central institution could also help those people — such as myself — who have an official position in government, but also hold independent critical views as Christians. What has come to be a familiar feature of most military machines is still wanted in the field of development assitance: centres for strategic studies which establish the criteria for working models, taking into account the given circumstances of power and the limits imposed by administrative rules and regulations. Here, a serious attempt could be made to make the everyday life of men, women and children in all parts of the world, rather than national political interests, the main consideration in planning a political action such as development assistance. Here would be the place for establishing guidelines for development promotion and for a critical analysis and re-interpretation of the statistics. Furthermore, certain questions could be answered for practical purposes, forgetting about all ideologies — such as what could be done to help societies in countries whose governments are in the hands of privileged minorities.

The churches will undoubtedly make enemies. In the past, they have made enemies for less weighty reasons. They have put up with schisms because they did not wish to make concessions when kings broke marriage rules. We need an institution to deal with the basic rules of a common development morality; an institution that is not committed to an ideology or culture, one which takes an open-minded attitude to everything that helps human advancement, however imperfect and small the steps may be. Apart from the above-mentioned study centre which should be given the right to request information and to be consulted, but no executive power vis-à-vis the churches' development agencies, and which should naturally employ a substantial number of experts from developing countries, there will be a need for regional development institutions, too. Here again, a dual system of independent study centres on the one hand and regional planning and executive bodies on the other would be an advantage.

Then we could safely leave it to further discussions in the individual regional institutions to decide how far non-church projects should profit from the financial assistance of the Church. Only regional, church-sponsored, though not monopolized-development agencies and institutions, supplemented by independent study centres, backed by ecumenical authorities, are able to effectively relieve the national agencies, establish links, arrange discreet projects, and relate the work of the churches to state and international projects, but also to the endeavours of private groups and progressive circles with a view to best effect.

Ye shall know them by their fruits, not merely by the goodwill shown and certainly not by the observance of competencies or the delimitations between groups.

The churches by themselves will not be able to change the social structures, but they can make a contribution if they extend their work to the whole society, not merely to their own communities. In the field of development assistance, the churches can show better than elsewhere that they do not exist for their own sake.

The UN Second Development Decade
and the Task of the Churches

by André Philip

Friends, I have been asked to speak about the Second Development Decade and about the attitude which the Church may take when faced by the crucial decisions presented by that Decade.

First of all I should like to make it clear that during the First Development Decade, which is drawing to its close, something really has been achieved, in spite of the disillusionment expressed on every hand. On the average the developing countries have increased their national income at the rate of 5 % per annum, which is twice as fast as our own countries in the middle of the 19th century when we began to be industrialized. We therefore must not adopt a critical, negative attitude towards what they have done so far; that attitude would merely strengthen the conservative elements who want to stop all forms of assistance to developing countries.

On the other hand, we cannot feel satisfied with what has so far been achieved and in my view the Pearson Report, interesting as it is and full of practical, positive suggestions, does not tackle the real problem. To aim at increasing the Gross National Product by 6 % (instead of 5 %), urging that 1 % of our own National Product (including 65 % of governmental aid) be devoted to development aid, and increasing our donations to development aid — all that is well and good but I do not think it is adequate. The point is not to do *more* than before. The point is to do something *different,* or in cases where we do the same things to do them *differently.*

I should like to give some general indications on this point before examining the rôle that can be played by the Churches. During the First Development Decade the mistake that was systematically made was to encourage a too-rapid process of industrialisation based on modern technology in some of the developing countries. Some countries were influenced by the Russian pattern. This reflected their leaders' desire for prestige, but most of all it reflected the interests of private investors, to whom it presented an opportunity to place their equipment in favourable conditions.

Private investment cannot be classified as aid, because it is really an attempt to obtain, or to maintain, control of the economic market. The predominant rôle which it has played has not succeeded in transmitting forms of technology adapted to the needs of the developing countries, nor in providing employment. In some cases it has even misdirected the economic development of the country by giving priority to the setting up of industries which require a great deal of capital but which employ very few workers, whereas the solution of the problem is exactly the reverse. Capital (which is scarce) must be economized and labour (which is abundant) must be employed. One of the mistakes made nearly everywhere was to set up conveyor-belts for assembling cars. These industries do not benefit the developing country at all, because the cost of the separate parts (which still have to be imported) is just as high as, if not higher than, the finished cars which that country imported before. When an investment is to be made, it is much more important to insist that the foreign investor entrusts the manufacture of separate parts to indigenous sub-contractors, for this will enable an industry to be gradually built up within the country.

In those cases where people are beginning to realise that it is a mistake to promote industrialization without considering what form it shall take and what it will cost, two things must be given priority and we should endeavour to give them first place during the Second Development Decade.

1.   In most of the developing countries 75 % to 80 % of the population consists of peasant-farmers. These peasant-farmers can take their destiny into their own hands, for development does not mean merely economic development; it means primarily the development of man, i. e. the assumption of responsibility by men where they are, starting from what they have. The development campaign must begin with the assumption of responsibility by the peasant-farmers themselves. Today great possibilities are opening up, since the advent of "the green revolution" (perhaps this expression is rather an exaggeration), i. e. since the discovery of selected seeds for rice and wheat which make it possible to double (or sometimes even to triple) production. We have noticed that peasant-farmers, even if they are illiterate, adapt themselves very quickly to the new methods and to the new kinds of seed and obtain results, under certain conditions.

The first condition, of course, is that they themselves may be able to benefit from the fruits of their efforts, and that these shall not be monopolized by some feudal landowner nor by a usurer or dealer who controls the market. In some countries this involves a complete revolution in the agricultural structures, for as long as they are dominated by feudalism (often tied up with foreign interests) all possibility for development is blocked.

In the other areas of the world a reorganization of the structures is the first essential, either by creating a system of cooperative credit or by nationalizing trade within each country, and above all by nationalizing foreign trade through marketing boards organized separately for each product. If this reorganization is carried out, if certain obstacles have been removed, and if the peasant-farmer has the feeling that he will benefit personally from his efforts, great possibilities are open today.

But another problem arises. The peasant-farmer who has a surplus will use part of it to feed himself better; he must be able to sell the rest in the town in exchange for consumer goods which enable him to improve his standard of living. He cannot do this unless there is sufficient buying-power in the town, and unless there are enough small industries (with simple machines) supplying the instruments and the consumer goods needed by the country.

2.   This brings us to the second priority: the growth of small enterprises (with simple machines), at first preferably in the larger market-towns, then in the urban centres. Industrialization on modern lines can then follow, but within a coordinated regional framework, for most of the developing countries (with a few exceptions, such as India and Brazil) are too small to be able to make the necessary investments for setting up a modern industry in their own country.

This approach which, in my view, is essential for the new decade of development presents a number of problems which already existed but have now become clearer, as well as some other problems which must be examined with fresh eyes:

— the need for increasing international aid to the developing countries;

— the need for coordinating that aid better through an international exchange of information; at present there is considerable overlapping and wastage — not so much among those who receive the aid but among those who give it;

— aid must be given "with no strings attached" (i. e. the developing country must not be compelled to purchase products from the country that is helping it), for studies have shown that when aid is tied, one-third of it goes to subsidize the exporters in the helping country, instead of giving real aid to the developing country. Aid must always be given without any strings attached, so that the developing country can effect purchases in other developing countries, or in any country which offers to sell goods 10 % or 15 % cheaper than the exporters in the helping countries. From now on at least 20 % to 24 % of all the aid given should be "untied", and this percentage should be progressively increased.

If the emphasis is placed (as it is bound to be) on aid to agriculture, which involves very little expenditure of foreign currency but a great deal of internal expenditure, part of the local cost should be covered by aid. This is indispensable if one wishes to participate effectively in rural training and rural development.

Aid must also include a new approach and new thinking in relation to what is still called in English "technical assistance". In French it is called "coopération technique". The word "coopération" represents a step forward. I am not sure whether such coopération is an absolute fact, but by creating a guilt-complex the use of the word "coopération" may prepare the way for a change in the situation. Too often, however, the experts who are sent out are not suited to the needs of the country. In all the industrialized countries the principle should be laid down that the technical colleges, agricultural training colleges, industrial colleges, engineering schools, universities, institutes for training economists, planners, statisticians, etc. should bear in mind (when selecting students) that 10 % of the persons trained should be made available to developing countries. In my view a technical assistant is usually useless during his first year in the developing country. He begins to be useful after that, when he has begun to understand something. He becomes useless again, or even harmful, after the fifth year, when he begins to get caught up in the administrative routine. It is time then for him to return home. This turnover in personnel is essential, and there should be an international pool of technical experts upon which any country could draw whenever necessary, in order to carry out the projects which it has itself chosen.

I must also mention another problem here. When a developing country has begun to advance, it must export. If it does not have access to a market, it will be faced by a deficit in its balance of payments. Too often its international trade is in the hands of foreign import-export firms which can and must be nationalized as soon as competent technicians have been trained to replace the foreign ones. But then the developing country comes up against the rules of an international market, upon which it has no real influence. Hence the need to try to organize the markets. Efforts have been made to do so during the First Development Decade. They proved successful in the case of some products. In the case of other products, however, these efforts came up against rival interests — not so much between selling countries and buying countries but between rival buying countries. This has caused the failure of many of the negotiations hitherto. In order to obtain a clear overall view of these problems, the UNCTAD Committee on raw materials has just proposed undertaking an international study on the structure of international trade, product by product, beginning with those products which seem at first sight to suffer from the exercise of power by some monopoly. It will be difficult to obtain the necessary information, but in my view UNCTAD's decision to undertake this task is an important one; for if the way in which international trade actually functions is shown up, that will be the way to prepare for its profound transformation, little by little.

However, the essential thing is not only to try to stabilize the prices of the goods at present sold by the developing countries, but also to purchase from them what they have not hitherto sold, even if this means that they begin to compete with us. Soon they will be selling wheat and rice and certain industrial products. Experience has shown that the policy pursued during the First Development Decade (the suppression of restrictions on quantity, negotiations to reduce tariffs, and the movement towards free trade) proved a complete failure owing to the opposition of the great combines and international commercial concerns which dominate the market.

Other measures must now be taken

1. The industrialized nations must take the decision to import a fixed percentage per annum from the developing countries; these imports will increase slightly every year as the national consumption increases, product by product. This would ensure real access to the market on entirely fresh lines.

2. In face of the big private combines with branches in many countries, large supra-national public bodies should be set up for a mixed economy, in the form of agreements between the governments of the consumer countries, organizing the whole process from the production of the raw material to its delivery to the consumer. Integration must not be confined to private enterprises, but must be undertaken by public enterprises.

3. It should be recognized that the First Development Decade proved the failure of the doctrine of economic liberalism and the doctrines of neo-classicism which have inspired all the international organizations and all the international conferences. The theory had been accepted without dispute that the free play of prices would ensure the best distribution of the product. It has become clear that that is not true. Nevertheless this theory still guides the thinking of the "establishment" and must be challenged. The problem is how to set up international development legislation which will change the existing structures in our own countries, in the under-developed countries and in the whole organization of the international market.

What can the Churches do in face of these problems?

During the Second Development Decade, as the emphasis is laid increasingly on agriculture and on the small industries with simple machines, the rôle of the churches, and of all the private, non-governmental and non-profit-making organizations, will assume primary importance. They can help to train agriculturalists, to organize cooperatives, to set up agricultural schools and vocational and technical schools. To this they can devote their resources and send out qualified persons.

As it becomes essential to create small or medium-sized concerns with simple techniques, the Churches will be in a better position than any other organization to encourage men to go out and set up small industries in those countries, on the understanding that after a certain time (10 or 15 years according to the case) these industries will be transferred to workers' cooperatives, whose members they have themselves trained. It will be difficult to get private budinessmen to do this, but the non-profit-making organizations (especially the Churches) could play a vital rôle here.

In the sphere of technical, agricultural or industrial training and in creating a reserve of experts who can be placed at the disposal of the developing countries, the Churches should try to act in cooperation with the non-governmental organizations (religious or secular), rather than as Churches. A number of enterprises, set up jointly by all the non-governmental organizations prepared to do so, should pool the funds which they devote to this purpose. Within the framework of a joint programme the Churches could then assume special responsibility for certain activities. These should be carried out on a regional basis in cooperation with the other non-governmental organizations working in the same area — in close contact, of course, which the Churches in those areas.

These are some indications of spheres in which the Churches can take direct action.

Lastly, at the opening of this Second Development Decade, the main rôle of the Church is to influence public opinion, to arouse people's awareness everywhere, to make them feel that it is not a question of technical assistance but of genuine cooperation. The Church must proclaim that everyone gives as well as receives, that everyone has much to learn, that the idea of "aid" must be abandoned as soon as possible, that the problem to be faced is that of the development of the whole world, which is really the same everywhere on different levels. It is obvious that the Europeans are "developed" in comparison with the Africans, but "under-developed" in comparison with the Americans. Europeans are in a good position to understand the problem and to register the reactions from both sides: understanding the American reactions in face of the under-developed countries, but also understanding the reactions of the under-developed countries when they discuss with the Americans. The problem is one and the same, the problem of world development; we must tackle it by setting up international legislation concerning development and working out a joint policy, in which all will participate in accordance with their wealth and their financial, technical and human resources. The real problem is the same problem which confronts Europe also: how to create a new civilisation, how to rediscover a sense of values, a sound plan, and human responsibility in order to cooperate in creating a responsible society administered at every level by persons who have at last become responsible.

The UN Second Development Decade and the Task of the Churches

by Robert Gardiner

The First Development Decade

The achievements and promise of the idea of a world-wide development decade are now capable of being summarised in a few propositions.

The developing countries, inclusive of oil-producing countries, registered an annual rate of increase in the real gross domestic product in the 1960s (or more precisely 1960—1967) less than the rates attained in the 1950s. Developing Africa, that is Africa excluding South Africa, in fact grew during the 1960s at an annual rate of only 4 per cent compared to the rate of 4.8 per cent attained in the earlier decade, 1950—1960. Likewise the countries of the Caribbean and Latin America recorded a fall in the overall rate of growth during the 1960s as compared to the 1950s.

The developing countries taken together, were all subject to the pressures of increasing population, and the rate of advance on a per capita basis declined from 2.4 per cent per year in the 1950s to 2.0 per cent per year in the 1960s. In Developing Africa, the annual rate of economic advance on a per person basis slowed down to 1.5 per cent from 2 to 7 per cent. In the Latin American region the corresponding figures were 1.8 and 2.3 per cent respectively. In East and Southeast Asia, the per capita increase in Gross Domestic Product (GDP) remained more or less constant at 1.8 and 1.9 per cent per year in the 1950s and the 1960s respectively. In both Developing Africa and East and Southeast Asia (excluding Japan), the largest disappointment was experienced in the agricultural field, where the rate of annual increase slowed down to 1.8 and 2.2 per cent as compared to the performance in the 1950s — namely, 3.7 and 3.2 per cent respectively. The performance in the 1960s was not merely smaller than the overall increase in the size of the population, but in most countries even smaller than the pace of enlargement in the population directly dependent upon agriculture. Or to put it alternatively, the bulk of the people in the developing world have experienced low rates of increase and in some cases even declining incomes in the course of the first Development Decade. They have not been able, for whatever reason, to become fair contributors to the process of national income enlargement and, in turn, have more or less failed to make their impact felt as consumers of non-agricultural goods and services. The gains that have taken place have too often accrued to the monetized, urban sectors. The rapid growth of urban populations, it would thus appear, has been as much a matter of the urban pull as it has been a matter of push from the rural areas.

I will seek to demonstrate the experience of peasants during the first decade from data* relating to Zambia, a country which recorded an annual increase of the Gross Domestic Product, in real terms of the order of 12 to 13 % after 1964:

Category of Income Earner	Approximate Numbers	Approximate Annual Earnings end 1968	Increase in Real terms since 1964
Peasant farmer	800,000	145 kwacha	3 %
Zambian wage earner outside mines	270,000	640 kwacha	52 %
Zambian mine worker	50,000	1,300 kwacha	35 %
Expatriate employee outside mines	22,000	4,170 kwacha	25 %
Expatriate employee, copper mines	6,000	7,600 kwacha	16 %

It might be instructive to catalogue the constraints, obstructions and problems which the developing world, notwithstanding several remarkable, but usually discontinuous cases of substantial economic advance, must by-pass, remove and solve. The inequities of the world trade systems; the inadequacy of domestic savings and investible resources; the steep rise in capital requirements for each job to be created; the concomitant rise in unemployment at the same time that wage and salary structures remain among the most unequal in the world; the limited stocks of skills and experience; the demographic pressures inherent in the reduction in the comparatively high death rates and the negligible operation of birth-inhibiting factors; and the inadequacies, in practice, of planning techniques. Perhaps underlying many

* Note: based on ILO, Report to the Government of Zambia on Incomes, Wages and Prices in Zambia: Policy and Machinery, p. 9. One Kwacha equals US $ 1.40.

of these issues, both within developing countries and in the developed countries is an attitude to development which might be summarized in the words of a hard-worked official: "We are still tackling twenty-year problems with five-year plans staffed with two-year personnel working with one-year appropriations."

The Second Development Decade

The United Nations system, after a vigorous debate in both specialist and non-specialist forums, has come to two major conclusions. In the first place, the moral imperative of economic growth in the poor countries is accepted. Secondly, it is felt that the record of performance of the 1960s is capable of being substantially improved upon. In quantitative terms, an average annual growth rate of 6 per cent for all developing countries taken together is now accepted as the basis on which technical studies should proceed.

In the context of Developing Africa, fulfillment of the targets implies an overall annual rate of economic advance which is 50 % higher. In per capita terms, we are thus thinking in terms of a rate of increase which is 2.33 times as high as the performance of the 1960s in Developing Africa, and somewhat smaller scales of increase in other parts of the developing world.

None of us in the United Nations system underestimates the scale of the task to be performed in the Second Development Decade. We are conscious of the problems left unresolved during the First Decade, the new political, economic and social stresses inherent in any process of rapid economic transformation, the uncertainty of internal and external capital sources and the diverse kinds of assistance which will be required.

The United Nations approach to the problems of the Second Development Decade might be summarized in the slogan or battlecry issued by the United Nations Economic Commission for Africa on its tenth anniversary: "A Venture in Self-Reliance in an Interdependent World". This slogan emphasizes the approach of the Administrator of the United Nations Development Programme, Mr. Paul Hoffman, that the technical assistance programme is not charity and that the notion of donor-recipient countries should be eliminated from considerations of international co-operation. Some of us believe that in the First Development Decade, mankind has endeavoured to learn the art of thinking internationally. Adlai Stevenson summed up this view in his speech to ECOSOC just before his death, when he said:

"We travel together, passengers on a little space ship all committed for our safety to its security and peace. We cannot maintain it half fortunate, half miserable; half confident, half despairing; half slave — to the ancient enemies of man — half free in a liberation of resources undreamed of until this day. No craft, no crew can travel safely with such vast contradictions. On their resolution depends the survival of us all."

The First United Nations Development Decade has been a period of learning to think in terms of one world; a taking up of opportunity, and for the new majority in the membership of the United Nations and its agencies a chance to adjust to sovereign independence.

We draw sustenance from the considerable interest shown by young persons in the affairs of the world as a whole. The various youth services such as the Peace Corps of the United States, the British Volunteer Programme of the United Kingdom, the two programmes of France, and the programmes of Belgium, Germany, Canada, Norway, Japan and others bear testimony to the desire and willingness of coming generations to play an active role in improving living conditions for all mankind. I believe that people who gain this personal experience will not need much convincing and that in future, when we have meetings of this kind, we shall not be stating the reasons why the Church and all individuals should give thought to the problems of poor countries.

The United Nations system and development tasks

It is now more than twenty years since the United Nations entered the field of providing technical assistance to underdeveloped countries. During this period, the world has noticed a new dimension in international relations: namely, the acceptance, however tenuously, of responsibility to assist the less developed countries to make some economic advance. We now understand a little more than we did twenty years ago about the problems and difficulties of development. We also now know that the ideas of economic "take-off" are not always literally and directly applicable to all countries and, in fact, may encourage the notion that the provision of aid is a short-term necessity.

The United Nations programme has undergone considerable changes. Nobody dreamt twenty years ago that the sum of $ 200 million could be raised annually by the United Nations to finance technical assistance programmes. The conversion of the world's community to the acceptance of such a programme is perhaps the greatest achievement of our century and for which we owe a great deal of gratitude to Mr. Paul Hoffman. The World Bank, too, is now involved in serving not only as a banker for granting loans but also as a source of assistance in undertaking pre-feasibility studies and in providing advice. The end of the First Development Decade, therefore, has rightly called for a reappraisal of the substance of multilateral programmes and the machinery for providing aid. I refer to the Jackson and Pearson reports.

The Pearson Report set out originally to examine the reasons why aid appeared to be less forthcoming and why it seemed that a feeling of disenchantment had descended on donor countries and their nationals. The Jackson Report has raised many questions about the effectiveness of the United Nations machinery and has proposed at the same time measures for increasing the capacity of the United Nations to use available resources to help poor countries. The desire to abolish poverty and misery is an old aspiration. What is perhaps new, in the changed circumstances of our scientific and technological age, is the crucial importance of success at the national and international levels, and the material prospects of attaining it.

In the course of the past decade, new organs have been developed to deal with aspects of poor countries' requirements, which aid alone cannot satisfy. I recall here the work of UNCTAD and UNIDO. The negotiations of UNCTAD have placed emphasis on the changing of the pattern not only of trade but of economic relations between the producers of primary commodities and the industrialized countries. UNIDO is charged with the search for ways and means of helping the inhabitants of poor countries to develop their industrial potential. And one should not forget that the United Nations Advisory Committee on the Application of Science and Technology aims at building up the necessary scientific knowledge and technical skills for the exploration and exploitation of natural resources.

A world programme of action is now being considered by the Committee on the Application of Science and Technology. Two other United Nations developments — the World Indicative Plan by FAO and the World Employment Programme by ILO — deserve attention. It appears that we have now reached a stage where worldwide programmes are formulated and accepted; in other words, some world instruments for the management of world problems have been forged.

The role of the churches

In the mid-1960s it was estimated that the supply of foreign manpower to developing countries amounted to 82,000 from bilateral technical assistance, 8,500 from communist countries, 8,000 under capital aid, around 100,000 from private foreign capital, and around 8,000 from multilateral technical assistance (mostly under UN programmes). Voluntary organizations (many of them church affiliated in one sense or another) supplied 15,000. In addition, out of 100,000 directly placed by religious organizations (almost entirely churches) in developing countries, between two-fifths and two-thirds were varyingly estimated to have been involved with technical assistance activities. I do not feel that even well-informed people are quite aware of the scale of activities undertaken by voluntary organizations, religious and non-religious.

The world at large is relatively unaware of the fact that the total flow of aid through non-governmental, non-profit organizations is in excess of $ 1,000 million every year. It is true that this figure includes funds put at their disposal by governments, and as such, the figure overstates the direct net contribution of these organizations. Nonetheless, it is clear that the role of the churches, even as providers of material support, is steady, significant and sizable by any quantitative and qualitative standards.

The areas covered by these organizations vary widely — and indeed enough is not known about them — but a mere recital of the activities of OXFAM, a non-religious organization which is to some extent supported by religious organizations, is impressive: provision of relief during "hunger months" and assistance in developing activities to end this crippling aspect of life in Africa; support of agricultural extension and fertilizer trials; fish farming, water conservation and irrigation;

95

the provision of facilities for agricultural training and agricultural credit; care of neglected groups work in the area of health and nutrition such as school feeding and innoculation campaigns, financial assistance to Medical Research — not to mention the rehabilitation of refugees and assistance to victims of civil strife (in the Congo and Nigeria).

I view the role of the churches as a substantial one in terms of their unique capacity to draw large numbers of dedicated people who have, on the record, an unusual capacity to adjust to the meagre facilities of small towns and villages in the developing world. I also view their role in a larger, community-wide sense, and not merely as a role related to those who are formally affiliated to Christianity or likely to become so affiliated, I regard the churches, with their extensive geographical spread, as inspirers and supporters of individual creativity in an era of large organizations, whether these be companies, government departments or others. It is in this context that I view the tasks of the churches in the Second Development Decade. I am aware that many, if not all, items in my list are being carried out somewhere right now. What is needed is a concerted approach, so that the sum of church activities may be seen to be larger than the total of the parts that make it up.

The tasks of the churches

a) The churches and allied organizations have a significant task earmarked for them particularly in small towns, rural areas and relatively inaccessible parts of many countries. By virtue of their flexible procedures, churches are well placed to select and carry out small projects at short notice which no centralized bureaucracy can handle with efficiency, and in the process, they are able to aid in creating a development-oriented local leadership. The kind of tasks I have in mind are the digging of wells or creating protected supplies of water, the building of roads, or the setting up of inexpensive all-weather warehousing and the introduction of new crops and more productive agricultural technology. The conspectus of needs and projects is, in essence, local and as such, has to be decided on the spot. Planners, understandably living in the capital town and working with macro-economic models and large projects, tend to forget or underestimate these small projects altogether.

96

b) As one who equates the process of economic development to the creation of capabilities — both in terms of organizational abilities and vocational skills — I feel that the role of the churches in education needs to be re-examined. Given the structure of employment opportunities in many developing countries, the emphasis has perhaps to shift to vocational education. In addition, the churches should become involved in the vocational training for adults, especially for those illiterate young men (and young women) who are being by-passed by new economic developments. For the young we need to reconsider the emphasis now placed on reading and writing and foreign languages which only the elite need.

c) In Developing Africa in particular, there is a widespread shortage of commercial and organizational skills. It is worth considering whether Church finance should not be directed to the creation of small enterprises — if need be — which may be eventually handed over, say after a period of trial on concessional terms either to willing and able individuals or, in suitable cases, to co-operatives. The Basel Mission in Ghana started the Basel Trading Company in Ghana a hundred years ago. I should like to visualize the organization of these activities in economically viable terms and not as acts of charity or merely education. Apart from the direct results, I would anticipate a wider result, as a large number of people get the opportunity of seeing from the inside what the operation of a small business or industry really involves and the possible translation of this firsthand lesson into several other enterprises.

d) In many cases, the churches in small towns and rural areas could help in the creation of special solutions — such as workers of the American Friends Service Committe helped in evoking in India when they worked up and tested out the designs for shallow tubewells. Likewise, the inexpensive hand pump designed with "wearing" wood parts (because mechanics or tools would not be available in the village, but a carpenter is available) instead of "steel" parts was a special solution. The need and scope for such solutions is very large.

e) Rapid urbanization is almost inherent in the process of economic development. In turn, urbanization is inevitably accompanied by changes in habits of living, stresses and vacuums in inter-personal relationships. Whereas I am not quite sure that these disintegrative tendencies can be completely obviated, there is certainly much that churches can do to alleviate the new, urban miseries to which we are becoming increasingly susceptible.

f) It has been argued even by some compassionate observers that "it is not always possible both to help the poorest people and promote development at the same time", because "they are the people who are least responsive to new ideas and techniques; any change could bring disaster and they have no spare resources with which to experiment". It is my feeling that until we can render this experience-based judgement invalid, we have not really begun the process of development. And, I would like to see that the reversal of the thesis covers not merely the poorest people, but all the neglected and disadvantaged groups, such as the young illiterate adults in urban areas, (domestic servants, unemployed school leavers) or people living outside of the transport network. The churches, with their unusual capacity to attract dedicated people and their unique geographical spread, could consider a systematic assault on this basic contradiction in current development experience and thinking.

g) Finally, I might be allowed to point out that the intellectual feedback from the grassroots understanding of development and technical assistance activities of the many thousands whom the churches have, directly and indirectly placed in the field is very limited. This must be changed, in co-operation with national and international agencies. We must be allowed to benefit, on a social scale, from the trials, errors and successes of the manifold activities already taking place under church auspices. We could establish a clearing house for information on development in the least developed regions.

The churches throughout the world have placed emphasis on the value of individuals. We have provided care for the sick and the needy, education and enlightenment. We have introduced skills in agriculture and trade. We have made an impact on the culture and ways of life of societies. This involves training and equipping those who are already alive and advising families on planning their numbers as well as the prospects for their children. Now that the world shares this human interest with us, we need to emphasize not only the humanistic aspects of our motives but also the divine inspiration which sustains us.

PART II:
Working Group Reports

Working Group I

The Debate about Development

I. *Development and Under-Development*

The process of western growth and expansion initiated in the 16th and 17th centuries, coupled with the Industrial Revolution, has produced and institutionalized in large areas of the world the patterns of relations which we refer to today as the condition of underdevelopment: the contrast between the wealth and power concentrated in some groups and nations, and the deprivation, weakness and lack of opportunity which are the lot of many others.

This process, the various stages of which are characterized by a rising level of technology with accompanying changes in the social and political institutions of many countries, is in itself a form of development. But it is an impersonal process which is propelled by its own internal dynamism, producing the results which we have before our eyes. Most striking among these results is the human condition of dependence and domination, of oppression and exploitation of the great majorities in large parts of the world.

But we rejoice in the fact that awareness and action are growing all over the world, aiming at liberation from these conditions, and the constitution of new patterns of relations among men and nations. We believe that this world struggle must include efforts to achieve not only radical economic change, but also profound transformation in the political, ideological and social systems dominant in the world today.

In this dynamic situation, churches are deeply affected in their own structure and in the life of their own members. They are called to a total engagement and to new action in society. Appeals to the churches have repeatedly been made, most recently at the Uppsala Assembly, and in the secular world there has been a new assessment of the results of action over the last quarter of a century. New lines of approach are now being formulated.

II. *Structure and Procedures*

We are therefore at the beginning of a difficult, but promising enterprise in ecumenical circles. In the first place, churches need to become more aware of the growing disparities between the poor, dispossessed and powerless, and the accumulators of wealth and power. Secondly, they must become aware that the challenges of development affect people around the world, both in "developed" and "developing" countries. Thirdly, at least a beginning has been made to tackle the consequences of the development process in its entirety — cultural, political, ideological, social and psychological. But for all this, the churches urgently need to deepen Christian understanding of the development process, to prepare themselves for meaningful participation in national, regional and world-wide action in development, and undertake specific church action in this vital and urgent field.

The greatest difficulties are inherent in the situation of social change itself. The breakdown of old patterns of society and the struggle to find new ones contains deep ambiguities. This produces uncertainty, the need to experiment, and different approaches — many of them supported with conviction and emotion. An earlier idea that economic change is dominant is now superseded by the conviction that development is a many-sided, all-pervasive process. At every point there is conviction that social change must lead to self-development and must produce, not increased dependence, but self-reliance.

Previous development theories and practice, preoccupied with economic determinants, seemed to suggest a fundamental division between "developed" and "underdeveloped", whereas today there is the emergence of a new understanding of development based upon new criteria of the social and the human, which makes the "developed" nations conscious of the spheres of underdevelopment in their own societies.

A major obstacle to development is the fact that the "developed" countries find it so difficult to see and accept the implication for their own societies of the search for new international political and social structures.

For this reason, and because of the fact that the centres of power and decision-making which determine the fate of many underdeveloped countries are located in the rich countries, a proportion of the money available for development should be spent in the "developed" countries for the purpose of bringing to light the facts about the ways and means by which this power is exercised. The churches have an important role to play in ensuring that this critical task is not neglected.

If it is true, as we have said, that all societies are "developing", then they (and their churches) must refuse to become mere "donors" or "receivers". They have to learn the real meaning of interdependence, i. e., how "developing countries" could become "donors" and vice versa. We recommend that this question be examined carefully and the churches of the industrialized nations be helped to think and move in this direction.

Underlying the whole discussion are different approaches which lead to different emphases both with regard to priorities and process. At this level the debate in ecumenical circles must be continued. While we are therefore not clear about the meaning and implications of development, we have to be engaged, acting on the best insights available, and continuing our quest for a fuller understanding of the goals.

III. *Dilemmas and Opportunities*

In the present situation, some major problems and dilemmas dominate the development process.

A. First, the question is seriously raised as to how there can be a meaningful collaboration between centres of wealth and power and the areas of poverty and weakness, both within and between nations. As the powerful countries seek to assist weak nations, the result may be either corrupting or crushing or both. The churches' development programmes must take account of this crucial problem, be responsive to different approaches and seek creative solutions to it. The criteria are self-determination as to goals and structures and a dynamic conception of social justice which alone can promote a satisfactory rate of economic growth and ensure progress toward self-reliance.

B. The foregoing concern emphasizes the need for change in national and international economic and political structures and processes, e. g.

international trade and investment. Otherwise, the very process of development tends to accentuate existing disparities and increase the power of the dominant group. The changes in structures and processes will vary sharply in different countries, and there is strong disagreement concerning the methods of change. Three basic issues are land tenure, the population explosion and the social effects of continuing rapid urbanization; but there are many others.

C. Rapid economic and social change generated by the development process has in fact produced disintegration of many forms of community life which gave people a sense of identity and belonging. The movement of urbanization and the movements from agrarian to industrial society is one of the chief causes of the collapse of the so-called "microsocial units". Therefore, alongside of the macro-changes (meaning the changes in the system as a whole), must come the efforts to build new units of community life that will give meaning to the search to many for dignity. Here is one of the significant areas for the church's effort in development. Through participation in the building-up of new micro-structures we can more effectively relate ourselves to structural change at the national level. Churches might, for example, experiment at various levels with projects which aid oppressed social groups to acquire the confidence to participate more effectively in the struggle for a more just social order.

D. There are basic contradictions between the search for coherent, dynamic and long-term development policies in all countries and the present preoccupation of most of our nations with increased military spending. The picture of so many nations devoting 30 — 40 %, or even more, of their national government budgets on armaments while programmes to meet the misery of urban masses in neglected slums and ghettoes are so inadequately financed, must haunt every Christian. Moreover, many in the new nations are convinced that much of this military spending is prompted by the determination of the powerful nations to maintain their authority against the aspiration for liberation.

IV. *Common Convictions*

As the foregoing points make clear, there is considerable divergence in the understanding of development. Nevertheless, there is agreement among us on certain aspects of the problem:

— development and social change are set in motion not only by the autonomous processes of science and technology, but are subject to the conviction and aspiration of men. Within this dynamic and complex process, Christian responsibility is to seek social and political institutions and processes that embody and enhance human dignity;

— movements of development and social change affect every nation, and none can escape. Many wish to control and judge these movements, whether by western capitalist or by socialist or other standards, but none of these standards are valid for all; free initiatives of self-development are essential for each. For this mutual help and cooperation are needed, and the ecumenical movement should do much more than at present to deepen and broaden the dialogue that makes this possible.

V. *The Ecumenical Process*

The problems connected with development cannot be solved once for all. Criteria for action should emerge from a process in which programmes can be worked out in response to the basic problems and different approaches to them. For this, the churches need to create national or sub-regional and international mechanisms of consultation, in which programmes and projects can be developed through a process built upon people of different view-points, different disciplines, and different experience. Thus, the debate about development should be incorporated into the process of decision-making and action. Moreover, work in development should not consist of isolated projects, but of interrelated programmes. These should be conceived and executed as a result of consultation and cooperation among varied groups and interests within the country or sub-region, and supported by cooperation among different agencies in the international community. Furthermore, the widest ecumenical cooperation and interfaith consultation are necessary, as well as cooperation with non governmental agencies.

The overall national, sub-regional and international mechanisms and processes which the churches create and use for their development programmes should be responsive to three factors:

— the actual social situation, carefully analysed and assessed;

— differing interpretations and responses to that situation; and

— basic agreements — as suggested above — in approach to work on development.

Working Group II

Policy and Procedures for Church Support to Development Projects

I. *Introduction*

a) We envisage that projects of development may be submitted for church support to the world-wide Christian community from all areas of the world, to tackle the problems of under-development which are in every country.

b) We understand that the primary place for decision-making about goals and strategies of development action by the churches, and about priorities for particular development projects is in the national situation considered in its regional context. We look to a sensitive dialogue within the whole ecumenical fellowship along the way to these decisions. The questions concerning criteria (see below) are designed to assist that dialogue.

II. *Appropriate National Organizations through which the Church might work in its Development Effort*

a) There is infinite variety in the national church situations which affect the way the Christian community can play its part in development — minority or majority situations, religious antagonisms, strength or weakness of human resources, degree of ecumenical penetration, vested interests, theological differences about the relation of the Church and world, all affect the question. It would therefore be wrong to expect or encourage one pattern of action for all. Sensitivity is required in discussions with local churches and councils of churches concerning the matter.

b) Four possible types of answer to the question may be envisaged:

i. The churches or National Council of Churches might handle the responsibilities for development effort themselves, seeking resources and strengthening their own structures and personnel as necessary.

107

ii. The churches or National Council of Churches might initiate the establishment of an autonomous body, within previously agreed relationships — specialized, primarily lay, comprising both Christians and when appropriate non-Christians, and being autonomous in the sense that it has direct relationship with the international ecumenical organizations in submitting projects for support.

iii. Churches or National Councils of Churches might join those national community organizations set up by Government initiative and related primarily to the work of intergovernmental agencies and work with and through them.

iv. More than one channel of responsibility might be recognized in a country — both a community-based organization and the National Council of Churches depending on the type of programme and the relationships which it involves.

III. *Appropriate Relationships in which the Church might involve itself in Development Projects*

a) Development effort being directed toward the ultimate welfare of the whole community in an area, cooperation between Church and other voluntary organizations within the community is to be encouraged. Programmes initiated by such independent local groups might be supported because of their pioneering character or their effect on the total development of the community. Sometimes official endorsement of the local church or autonomous agencies channelling support may not even be required and other ways for testing the validity of these programmes may be sought at the local level by the international ecumenical agencies.

b) National Governments and Inter-governmental agencies.

i. While there will be reluctance in certain political situations to become tied to governments, in other situations the churches are in fact relating themselves to the national development planning of their governments, and must often do so to be effective instruments for national development. In minority situations, to do so may be an important bridge-building strategy for the Church.

ii. Cooperation with inter-governmental agencies, especially of the UN development system, operating in a country offers a further field for effective development effort, and one which opens the local community to the sense of belonging to a world-wide community.

iii. Cooperation with both governments and inter-governmental agencies is not usually a matter of simply supplying church funds; it should try to involve the participation of the local church in planning or in operation through the use of personnel or otherwise. Operational cooperation can take many forms, e.g.:

— to help to make a project more indigenous by encouraging the local community to participate in it and accept the changes that it may bring about;

— subsidiary projects of a social kind in the wake of large constructional undertakings leading to mass movement of people;

— follow-up programmes, spreading the benefit of the programme to the population.

— Sometimes the local church or autonomous agency can even serve as the operational arm for a particular project.

iv. While working cooperatively with governments, there is also a need for the Church to work independently in order to undertake pioneering tasks not yet taken up by governments in their development plans, and to take calculated risks in setting up projects to prove new techniques.

c) The churches' own programmes of development will still be necessary, whatever organizations or patterns of cooperation develop. Some types of programmes in this category are:

i. Programmes for the development of Christian leadership for participation in development projects, for the development and use of church assets for development purposes and for the establishment of self-reliant national Christian service agencies.

ii. Programmes reflecting what are regarded as distinctive Christian perspectives concerning man in the particular national community.

IV. *Some of the Criteria which help to describe Development Work*

a) We recognize the following types of programmes as falling within the description of development work appropriate for church action:

i. Programmes which promote social justice including programmes for the study and development of methods of non-violent change of structures, and programmes for the support of actions aimed at the change of structures.

ii. Programmes which promote the self-reliance of the community, and encourage the participation of people in the process of their own development.

iii. Programmes which promote economic growth of the community creating social imbalance.

iv. Programmes which help to provide new creative patterns of life for communities and groups whose lives have been disrupted by the effects of economic growth or the injustice resulting from it, or due to social or religious factors.

v. Programmes which help to reconcile estranged groups and build bridges between separated groups in the interests of a more integrated society.

b) We recognize two methods of operation:

1. Programmes of direct implementation,

2. Programmes of leadership formation, and community education.

c) We recognize the following as necessary conditions for the carrying out of effective development work.

1. There must be adequate technical competence in preparation and implementation of the programme.

2. There must be an adequate supply of competent dedicated local leadership and personal and other resources to ensure the continuance or completion of the work started with support from Christian communities abroad.

3. The programme must indicate its objectives and show evidence that there is a reasonable chance of achieving them, taking into account calculated risks.

V. *Methods of Handling Funds*

We recommend the establishment of a Central Fund for Development, which would complement the presently existing methods of funding projects ecumenically.

The board should be composed of members from countries where funds are raised and where projects are operated.

The Fund could be used among other ways for assisting programmes of development in the following ways:

a) For making initial grants to projects while financing is being sought through earmarked contributions.   .

b) For making block grants to national agencies without allocation to specific projects, but within carefully defined agreed criteria.

Structure and Organisation of Ecumenical Assistance to Development Projects

The establishment of a structure which is capable of responding adequately to the new demand for development will require boldness in imagination, freshness in approach and relevance in its organization. The soundness of this new structure will depend upon:

i. adherence to and implementation of its underlying principles;

ii. carrying out the functions derived from these principles;

iii. a workable structure with authority, relationships, resources and staff sufficient to discharge these functions, and

iv. becoming the central unit in the World Council of Churches where all programmes and projects related to development are coordinated in the light of the findings of this Consultation and of insights arising from experience in the field, and from the work of other relevant units in the World Council of Churches and the knowledge available from governmental, inter-governmental and academic sources.

I. *Principles*

Whatever the structure of the organization itself, it must be designed to assume the adherence to, and implementation on a multilateral basis of at least the following principles:

i. *Human development* — enabling both persons and societies to realize the full potential of human life in social justice, self-reliance and economic growth;

ii. Provision for comprehensive *programmes* and for specific *projects* seen in the perspective of national or regional needs;

iii. The capacity to assure ready response and quick action;

iv. Sensitivity to the relationships between agencies in developing and developed countries;

v. Openness and flexibility to *cooperation* with other organizations and to *change* as new circumstances and relationships may require;

vi. Distribution of power so that the decision-making process is fully shared at all levels, recognizing that the primary responsibility for development programmes and projects rests at the local, regional or national levels;

vii. Ability to adapt insights, methods, structures and perspectives by consultation at all levels, so that there will be coordination in planning and action in decision;

viii. Utilization of experts to insure the viability of programmes and projects, and

ix. Stimulating voluntary efforts by the churches and people in the development process; local commitment to and participation in any programmes or projects to the greatest extent possible.

II. *Functions*

In putting these principles into practice, the following functions should be fulfilled:

i. *Reflection and forum* on the meaning of development and the church's role in it; *continuous reassessment* of the situation in world development and the strategy required;

ii. *Leadership* in providing:
a) motivation;
b) development education;
c) information; and
d) action leading to social change
in both developed and developing countries;

iii. *Activity in selected sectors:*

— as a match-maker, bringing together needs and resources, human, material and technological; and providing a genuine confrontation between the partners in the development process;

113

— as a catalyst or initiator, for multilateral planning and action; and

— as a partner in regional, national or international plans of other entities engaged in development.

This will require planning and research, feasibility studies, support and services, and evaluation;

iv. Responsibility for *mobilization* of human and financial resources for development; and

v. Relations with other relevant bodies in the U.N. system and in the governmental and non-governmental fields.

III. *Structure*

Preamble

A pressing need exists for a new structure in the World Council of Churches to:

a) give expression to the urgency with which the Council must approach world needs for development;

b) coordinate the many development concerns of the different parts of the Council;

c) think through the fundamental task and strategy of the churches and the World Council as they focus on the challenges of development;

d) assure that the Council's methods of operation in the development field are suited to these challenges; and

e) open and develop possibilities of cooperation with non-member churches, including the Roman Catholic Church.

The structure proposed means that we seek to focus the concern for development in the World Council in such a way that it will have its impact on and will finally affect all programmes and projects in all units of the WCC.

A. Therefore, provisions needs to be made for:

i. *A Commission on the Churches' Participation in Development Programmes* (CCPD), its membership consisting of 20 to 25 persons, all of whom shall be experts in development disciplines or experienced in the church involvement therein. At least one half of the members of the Commission shall be from developing areas and one half from developed areas;

ii. The Commission to have an Executive Committee of not more than 7 members;

iii. A staff responsible to the Commission;

iv. The Commission to be directly related and accountable to the Central Committee of the World Council of Churches.

B. The *Mandate* should include:

i. Study, reflection and analysis of the churches' role in development, bringing to bear in its strategies and programmes insights suggested in item 4 of the Introduction;

ii. Assisting all efforts in development information and education and promotion of it in all parts of the world;

iii. Policy coordination in the choice and execution of development programmes and projects (see Functions in II, 3 to 5, above);

iv. The coordination of all the World Council of Churches' programmes bearing on development efforts and of its share in SODEPAX; and

v. Within the World Council's policy to secure a World Development Fund to enable it to carry out its mandate.

C. *World Development Fund*

The World Development Fund will be the responsibility of the Commission on the following understanding:

i. The money will be substantially distributed among the various regions and spent only on the initiative of the regions in terms of the Commission's strategy;

ii. The Commission will not be responsible for the detailed implementation of the agreed project but that implementation would be committed by the Commission, with agreement of the regions, to agencies, of which DICARWS would be one;

iii. A small portion of the Fund would be used for the immediate administration cost of the Commission;

iv. The raising of the World Development Fund and the funding of DICARWS' projects should be presented to the churches in a coordinated way.

D. *Ways of Work**

DICARWS and other units of the WCC are already engaged in development projects in conversation with churches and will be continuing this work raising funds for their support. As the Commission develops its understanding of development strategy DICARWS and the other units of the WCC will be influenced by the Commission's thinking.

Within the framework of its basic policy, the Commission shall seek to delegate to relevant bodies different aspects of its work. This would mean in addition to its own direct activities that *by agreement with* the WCC units and the agencies concerned, it would seek:

i. To arrange for the carrying out of programmes and projects by DICARWS or other units of the World Council of Churches or other agencies;

ii. To arrange for the possibility of loans and investment by ECLOF, or other agencies;

iii. To arrange for technical services by ACTS or other agencies as may be needed; and

iv. To arrange for aspects of its study, education and information work to be done with or by SODEPAX.

---

* In respect to ways of work, attention should be paid to the section on counterpart groups in the Report of Working Group IV.

Technical Assistance for Church Sponsored Development

I. *Nature and Types of Technical Cooperation*

Present patterns of technical cooperation hinge on the fallacious idea of transferring knowledge and techniques from the materially developed countries to less developed countries, on the assumption that these techniques are of high quality and suited to the needs of the latter. Nevertheless, it is easy to demonstrate that these patterns may have inherent defects such as the following:

i.   A high amount of wastage and loss is due to inadequate understanding of ecological and human conditions in "recipient" countries. Advanced techniques, as they are usually designed for temperate zones, may be unsuited to tropical and subtropical areas. Moreover, they may be socially counter-productive, as for example those based on automation which increase unemployment and short-circuit the use of more appropriate or intermediate technologies.

ii. A passive and often alienating imitation of models prevailing in dominant countries is fostered in developing countries, especially in the social, educational and cultural fields. The fetish of certain techniques, experience and philosophy from industrialized countries may create obstacles for fruitful cooperation between those countries and others in process of development.

iii. Markets subject to control by dominant nations are frequently created, which may be neither politically nor economically acceptable to developing countries in the perspective of social justice.

iv. Experts and technicians who do not have appropriate attitudes, or who are unable to adjust to local conditions, customs and language often fail to transfer knowledge adequately to achieve desirable changes. Frequently they reflect vested interests either personally or of the agency that employs them, thinking more in terms of self promotion than the welfare of the recipients.

These problems lead to the necessity of *stimulating and promoting technical creativity* in the developing countries. Likewise, administrative and managerial talents must be encouraged.

Creativity is everywhere a potential; in several developing countries it is an actual reality. However, what it lacks is organized stimulation and support from bodies independent from established institutions; many of whom persist in imitating foreign techniques for prestige reasons. The purpose of this policy would be to awaken the talents, self-respect, dignity and critical spirit of nationals, both technicians and others, and ensure their participation in the construction or reconstruction of their societies. It would demonstrate a better use of human resources, that may even put a brake on the present accelerating brain drain and loss of talent from under-developed to developed nations. The underlying philosophy is that of transformation of culture and society without losing the riches of historical self identification, by releasing the full dynamic potential of that society.

Therefore, the basic principle to be adopted is that, wherever possible, solutions to local problems should be found in developing countries themselves, using local personnel, initiatives and materials.

To promote this the following steps are advocated.

i.   Find and employ local technicians in the developing countries concerned that could wrestle with the problems.

ii. Stimulate the creativity of such local, morally committed, technical personnel by giving them enough resources and support to proceed independently.

iii. Stop promoting exported techniques, knowledge, equipment, that prove to be esoteric to, or ineffective for real development, or mainly responsive to artificial pressures of prestige considerations. One of the basic obstacles to realizing this emphasis on local elements is the overwhelming preoccupation with buildings and their expansion. This is frequently due to the donor agencies' stipulation that funding is only available for capital costs. An honest approach to the development of human resources necessitates a change in this policy and would require that adequate funds be released for the support of such development programmes which may not readily achieve self-support.

II. *Organization and Implementation of Projects*

The organization and implementation of projects should be conceived within programmes guided by one overall criterion: that of pursuing social justice and transforming unjust social and economic structures. For this reason development agencies of the Churches should be manned at all levels by persons animated by the highest ideals of social service, capable of responding to and catalyzing the aspirations and actions of the local common people, in order to promote significant, not marginal, change, i. e. transformations that break the bonds of traditional dependence and exploitation.

On the World Council level, one of these agencies is ACTS, the Advisory Committee on Technical Services.

The following mandate of ACTS seems to provide a suitable framework, when interpreted in the direction of the principles discussed above:

Aim: It shall provide or help to make available technical assistance for projects referred to it primarily by WCC and church-related agencies.

Functions:

i. *At the pre-implementation stage*
   a) technical feasibility of projects
   b) general assessment of projects

ii. *During implementation*
   a) technical assistance for project implementation
   b) ongoing evaluation

iii. *At the post-implementation stage*
   a) evaluation of projects

In carrying out these functions, ACTS must have access to relevant information and pertinent data. It will also inevitably contribute towards evolving general criteria and a strategy for development projects undertaken by the churches."

With a view to facilitating coordination by promoting improved administrative procedures, the WCC is requested to convene urgently a Working Party on harmonizing the project application questionnaires of church and, if possible, secular agencies.

Project Registration

In addition to this, negotiations should be inaugurated with CIDSE (International Cooperation for Socio-Economic Development), and other agencies, to establish a coordinated or joint registration of church-related projects.

Counterpart Groups

Those directly responsible for the carrying out of development projects should be, at the same time, responsible for their administration.

However, taking into account the need for national or regional planning and coordination as well as the determination of adequate priorities, it is recommended that national or regional partnership or counter-part groups of an independent nature be set up. Wherever possible such groups should be established through national or regional initiative, so as to ensure national or regional coordination and strategy in the development performance of the churches. The latter recommendation should be implemented on an experimental basis in a limited number of countries and be re-examined after some time.

While the nature of such counter-part bodies has to be adopted to the situation in each country or region, the following guidelines should be kept in mind:

a) they should be ecumenical wherever possible;

b) they may or may not be related to NCCs;

c) they should be composed of members chosen for technical competence with representation of youth and women; marginal or disadvantaged groups should also be represented.

d) these groups would be expected to initiate study and research into national and regional priorities for the churches in development and not simply to react to project initiators;

e) they should relate to national development plans whenever appropriate and cooperate with secular agencies involved in technical cooperation.

Financing

The cost of the setting up and the functioning of national or regional counterpart bodies as well as the provision of technical assistance should be charged, at least partially, through a project tax system, which would form a special account to be administered internationally by an appropriate body. This system should prevail as long as no acceptable other system of financing is available which guarantees their independence and their technical qualifications.

Coordination and Liaison Relationships

The WCC agencies for Development should explore the possibility of employing regional coordinators to serve as catalysts for local situations and to act in liaison between counterpart groups and the WCC. Moreover, from time to time, seminars should be organized either nationally, regionally or internationally, to establish an exchange and dialogue between those responsible for projects and national/or regional counterpart groups, between international or national church agencies from advanced countries and national or regional counterparts.

The churches and the WCC should, as far as practicable, make use of the specialized national and international Christian bodies (agriculture, nutrition, cooperatives, work by and for women, etc.) which have been established for the purpose of rendering technical services to churches. We urge that these bodies continuously reassess their procedures and staffing to the basic premises of technical cooperation set out above.

III. *Research and Evaluation*

The dubious experience of the Development Decade gives clear evidence that churches, both in the developing and the developed countries, must undertake a searching and critical review of whether their project and programmes promote fundamental social justice, or are only marginal palliatives which may actually prevent profound change.

To generate this basic review, we urge a number of steps to provide long range reflection.

i. An increasing number of projects and programmes must be more systematically evaluated.

ii. Emphasis should be put on *action* research, i. e., research related to informed and self-critical decision-making.

iii. Research and evaluation should not be oriented exclusively to single isolated projects, but should raise questions of a total strategy. This will require greater attention to non-church efforts and governmental plans. Basic research on the churches as institutions in transforming societies is also necessary.

iv. Projects should not be reviewed only in relation to technical criteria. Evaluation should raise questions of social values, such as their "self-help", "pioneering", "social awareness" and other qualities.

v. Research and evaluation must be oriented to the promotional concerns of the churches as such, but to their technical and social efficacy. This means, among other things, that failures as well as successes must be reviewed.

vi. Some important types of research are self-studies, information systems on projects, and case studies, which combine both the cross-sectional and the historical approaches.

vii. It is urged that the documentation service of the WCC continue to explore ways and means of cooperation with national, international and other significant bodies, working on development questions.

Working Group V

The Mobilization of Funds

I. *Preamble*

Though the subject for this Group's deliberations was the mobilization of funds, the consensus of the group is that other forms of resources need to be included in our considerations. Furthermore, our concern for development is based upon the Christian's understanding of the basic unity and solidarity of all mankind and therefore by development we mean nothing less than world development in terms of social justice, self-reliance and economic growth of all people.

II. *What are the Resources to be mobilized?*

What then are the resources that need to be mobilized? In every society there are, besides monetary resources, both public and private, natural resources, such as soil, water, raw materials, etc., and human resources, both individual manpower, skilled and unskilled, and groups, organized and unstructured, of men, women and youth. Technical knowledge and know-how in many specialized fields, must also be counted amongst resources to be mobilized and communicated for the purpose of wholesome development of human society everywhere.

III. *How are the Resources to be mobilized?*

What are the means by which these resources may be mobilized for the ultimate objectives of world development? We would suggest the following:

i. The exchange and dissemination of relevant information with regard to the existing needs through personnel exchange and by the effective use of all media of mass communication: radio, TV, daily press, magazines, books, etc.;

ii. Education, through formal education of children and youth and through adult and community education of various sorts;

iii. Political action along with other groups actively interested in world development so as to influence national governments, government institutions, parties, private enterprises, trade unions, student groups, etc., to redeploy their resources and re-evaluate their policies in order to further world development.

iv. Participation in and support of programmes executed by the UN Development system for the purpose of world development, such as the Freedom from Hunger Campaign. In particular, during the Second UN Development Decade, churches should actively be involved in order to ensure that the political will necessary for the realization of development aims is created.

v. Critical self-examination by the churches of their own resources of personnel, property and funds, which is further detailed below.

IV. *How much should be mobilized by the Church?*

At the Fourth Assembly of the WCC in Uppsala, the following recommendations were made:

— there should be "a re-examination of the basic objectives of church programmes and budgets in the light of the urgent tasks of nation building in developing countries";

— "every church should make available for development aid such proportion of its regular income as would entail sacrifice, this amount to be in addition to the amounts spent on mission and other programmes";

— the churches "should explore how international foundations could be set up through which endowments and other church funds may be responsibly invested for development";

— "the individual Christian is called . . . in developed countries, to make available for development aid, by means of a voluntary self-tax procedure, a percentage of his income related to the difference between what his government spends in development aid and what it should spend for this purpose".

The Uppsala recommendations point out that action with regard to development does have a major priority for the Church. From this

124

follows that we cannot speak just in terms of the mobilization of additional resources for this purpose. That, in fact, would mean that development would get only a marginal priority. Therefore, churches giving a major priority to development should redeploy their present resources.

Several churches seem to have taken the Uppsala recommendations seriously. However, many churches have not yet taken any decision along these lines.

We are aware that one of the possible causes for this delay lies in the formulation "such proportion of its regular income as would entail sacrifice". It is indeed difficult to define what this means exactly. In any case, it does not mean that every church makes available the same percentage of its regular income: there are both rich and poor churches, there are churches which get governmental support and churches which are supported by the voluntary contributions of their members, there are churches with an annually increasing income and churches whose income is decreasing.

However, we urge that in any case decisions be taken soon. For that purpose, we propose a procedure of decision-making in stages, as to the resources which the churches should make available for use within the new structures recommended by this Consultation.

i.   We propose all churches accept now as an objective for their giving in 1971 a minimum of two per cent of their regular income from all sources. (This is about the precentage decided upon already by some churches.)

ii. Further, we recommend that part of such and other resources for development be made available for a World Development Fund (as proposed by Group III). In order to initiate such a fund, we propose at least 10 million dollars for 1970.

iii. At the same time, in each church a fundamental and open discussion should take place about priorities for church action and about the necessary redeployment of funds, manpower and so on, to make these priorities operational. In this discussion, all people should be able to participate. Not only a redeployment of the annual income of all church bodies (contributions of individuals to churches, capital income and other income) should be taken into consideration, but also a redeployment of the church capital which is invested in land, buildings, investment portfolios, etc. (This follow the WCC Central Committee decision taken in Canterbury to set aside part of its reserves for the struggle against racial discrimination.) The discussion should lead to decisions on long-term commitments whereby the two per cent should be considered as nothing more than a minimum for 1972 and the following years.

Apart from the redeployment of the Churches' financial resources, the individual Christian should be challenged by information-education campaigns to contribute, on a continuing basis, funds for development. Those contributions (through self-tax movements for instance) should aim not only to provide funds but even more to express the individual's commitment to and understanding of development efforts.

V. *Utilization of Funds*

The funds raised should be used for two types of action, both of which are of equal importance:

a) for the financing of development projects, and

b) for educational programmes, the mobilization of public opinion and the financing of political action, especially in the affluent countries, to foster world cooperation for development. The proportion of total resources to be spent on these activities will vary from country to country, and may initially be as high as 25 per cent. (In this category will also fall the financing of the central work of the WCC in this field, because we think that the WCC, for example, the Division of Ecumenical Action, should fulfil a major role in stimulating and coordinating these actions.)

VI. *Governmental Funds for Development through Church Channels*

At present several governments, particularly in Europe, are accepting church projects for support. They recognize that the church is able to reach the grassroots in many countries.

For this purpose both the Roman Catholic and Protestant Churches in Germany and Holland have established separate offices for the preparation and presentation of church projects to their Government. In other countries Government contributions go through the existing channels of Mission and Service Agencies.

It is estimated that $ 10 million to $ 15 million annually comes from this source for the Protestant Churches, mostly going through bilateral channels, part of it through the World Council of Churches and part of it through the Lutheran World Federation. We endorse this as a continuing policy of the WCC in development programmes.

PART III:

Actions of the General Secretary
and the Executive Committee
of the World Council
of Churches

Letter of the General Secretary

To the Member Churches of the World Council of Churches,
Service Agencies, and Mission Boards

My dear friends,

Following a direction set by the Uppsala Assembly and confirmed
by the Central Committee at Canterbury, the Executive Committee
of the World Council of Churches, meeting in Geneva February 16
to 20, made very important decisions on the recommendation of the
Montreux Consultation on Ecumenical Assistance for Development
Projects, which I wish to present for your serious consideration.

First, the Executive Committee has approved the establishment
of a Commission on the Churches' Participation in Development. I
enclose for your information the document setting out the detailed
plans for this Commission. The Executive Committee members and
the staff as a whole warmly support this proposal and regard it as a
major step forward in the work of the World Council. The Montreux
Consultation spoke of development as a need confronting all countries
and societies. It identified the main thrust of the Churches' involvement
in development programmes as the promotion of social justice and
self-reliance.

Second, I draw your attention to the fact that the Executive
Committee endorsed the consultation's appeal that all member churches
contribute not less than 2 % of their total income for development
programmes and projects around the world, including those in their
own country. While this appeal is expressed in financial terms, we are
acutely aware that it implies a radically new understanding and
commitment by the Churches and their members.

Third, while it is quite clear that every Church will make its own
decisions as to the channels through which it will contribute to
development, I draw your attention particularly to two closely related
channels within the World Council itself, namely the Ecumenical
Development Fund and the Division of Inter-Church Aid, Refugee
and World Service.

The Ecumenical Development Fund is described in the enclosed document. You will readily recognise that this calls for very new procedures — the making available of undesignated funds for spending through decentralised decision-making agencies. It is hoped that at least $ 10 million will be contributed to this fund in 1970.

The Division of Inter-Church Aid, Refugee and World Service has adapted its procedures to allow it to handle special development projects for which funds can be specifically designated. Details of the first list of such projects, which will certainly relate to all continents, will be available shortly.

May I, in conveying these decisions to you, urge you to give them your early attention. Naturally, we will be ready to provide any further information you may require. I look forward to hearing from you.

Eugene Carson Blake
General Secretary

Geneva, 25 February 1970

132

Commission on the Churches' Participation in Development (CCPD)

Proposal as approved by the Executive Committee
at its meeting in Geneva, February 16—20, 1970

A. *Preamble*

There is a pressing need for a new structure in the World Council of Churches in order to:

i. give expression to the urgency with which the Council must approach world needs for development;

ii. think through the fundamental task and strategy of the churches and of the World Council of Churches as they focus on the challenges of development;

iii. coordinate the many development concerns of the different parts of the World Council of Churches;

iv. open up possibilities of cooperation with non-member churches, including the Roman Catholic Church in the field of development; and

v. facilitate collaboration with governmental, intergovernmental and voluntary agencies involved in development.

(This proposal is made recognizing that it may be altered in the light of the findings of the Structure Committee of the World Council of Churches.)

B. *Principles guiding the work of the Commission*

i. Development should be seen as the process by which both persons and societies come to realize the full potential of human life in a context of social justice, with an emphasis on self-reliance; economic growth being seen as one of the means for carrying forward this process.

133

ii. The approach should be one which takes into account development needs in all parts of the world.

iii. Because the primary responsibility for development programmes and projects rests at the local, national and regional levels, there should be distribution of power in the decision making process.

iv. There should be a recognition of the importance of maximum participation by the local community in development work, and of the potential of the church to stimulate such voluntary efforts.

v. There should be a recognition of the need for ready response and quick action.

vi. There should be a comprehensive approach in which reflection, planning and action are held together.

vii. As the needs of societies and the approach to the development process are varied, there should be openness and flexibility in methods of operation.

viii. Provision should be made for the utilization of experts to ensure the competence and viability of programmes and projects.

ix. There should be a bringing together of needs and resources, human, material and technological; and a provision for a genuine confrontation between partners in the development process.

x. There should be a maximum of openess and flexibility to cooperation with other Christian organizations and churches at present outside the World Council of Churches' membership including the Roman Catholic Church; and a willingness for changes in structures and ways of work as new circumstances and relationships may require.

xi. There should be a recognition of the importance of collaboration with secular agencies, religious groups and men of other faiths involved in development work.

xii. There should be an openness to collaboration with governments and with intergovernmental agencies, particularly those of the United Nations development system.

C. *Functions*

i. Reflection, study, consultation and the provision of a forum for discussion about the meaning of development and the churches' role in it.

ii. Responsibility for providing information and assistance to churches in the field of education and action leading to changes necessary for development.

iii. Assisting the various units of the World Council of Churches, its constituency and related bodies, in the formulating of policy and strategy for their involvement in development programmes and projects.

iv. Coordination of all World Council of Churches programmes and activities bearing on development efforts and of its share in the work of SODEPAX (Joint Committee on Society, Development and Peace).

v. Responsibility for facilitating cooperation in the field of development between the World Council of Churches, and non-member churches, voluntary agencies, and governmental bodies; and, in cooperation with the CCIA, with the intergovernmental agencies of the United Nations Development System.

vi. The making available of technical services for development programmes and projects.

vii. To facilitate the establishment of local, national and regional groups with similar aims and functions as the CCPD.

viii. The operation of an Ecumenical Development Fund.

— The purpose of this fund is two-fold:

a) To ensure that national, regional and sub-regional groups have both the initiative and the final say about the utilization of funds for development work in their respective areas.

b) To ensure that programmes of development supported and carried out by the churches are those in which the main emphasis is given to the promoting of social justice and self-reliance.

135

— The Fund will be used in the following ways:

a) The major portion will be made available to regional, sub-regional and national groups with the same general strategy as that of the CCPD. It will be used according to purposes and criteria mutually agreed upon between the CCPD and the body to which the grant is made.

b) The Fund may also be used to support:

— programmes of development in those areas where no groups such as those described above exist, and

— programmes of development which, because of their geographical or functional nature require financing from an international source.

In either case, funds may be made available, for the support of projects and programmes, to appropriate national or international agencies, including the Division of Inter-Church Aid, Refugee and World Service and other units of the World Council of Churches.

c) The administrative costs of the CCPD will be a charge on the Fund.

D. *The Commission*

It is proposed that:

i. The Commission have a membership of 20 to 25 persons all of whom shall be experts in development or experienced in church involvement in development programmes.

ii. At least one half of the members of the Commission shall be from the "developing" areas and one half from "developed" areas.

iii. The Commission will have an executive committee of not more than seven members.

iv. The Commission will be directly related and accountable to the Central Committee of the World Council of Churches.

v. The Commission will meet at least once a year. Its executive committee will meet at least twice a year.

vi. Consultants from other units of the World Council of Churches or related bodies may be invited to the meetings of the Commission according to the agenda, for discussions with the Commission.

E. *The Staff of the Commission*

In order to perform its task, the Commission will have a Director and a supporting executive staff who will fulfil the following functions: Study Coordination; Development Education; Documentation; Development Fund.

F. *Relationships*

There will be close relationships between the Commission and the various departments and divisions of the World Council of Churches involved in development work, both at the committee and staff level. The precise nature of these relationships remains to be worked out, but the following needs to be said at the present moment.

i. At the committee level.

a) Appropriate contact should be maintained between the CCPD and the Committee of DWME, DEA and Church and Society on matters of mutual interest.

b) The Advisory Committee for Technical Services will report to the Central Committee through the CCPD.

c) The report of the SODEPAX Committee will be presented to the Central Committee through the CCPD.

d) As the Commission has an overall responsibility for policy and strategy in development matters and as it is agreed that the Division of Inter-Church Aid, Refugee and World Service will continue to work with development projects, provision will be made for mutual reporting between the CCPD and that Division on matters of mutual concern.

e) Similarly, in so far as ECLOF is involved in loans or investment for development projects, there will be mutual reporting between it and the CCPD on matters of strategy and policy in this field.

ii. At the staff level

a) The Staff Working Party on Development will continue to be the forum in which there is mutual consultation among the staff of the World Council of Churches on matters of development policy and strategy.

b) The Director of ACTS will be administratively responsible to the Director of the CCPD.

c) The Director of the CCPD will be the senior WCC staff officer of SODEPAX.

d) There will be a close relationship between the staff of the CCPD and the staff of the Division of Inter-Church Aid, Refugee and World Service, in the handling of development projects. There will be a coordinated approach in raising funds for development projects approved by DICARWS and the Ecumenical Development Fund of the CCPD.

Appendices

Appendix I

Summary of the Debate at Montreux
by Reinhild Traitler

The question raised over and over again was whether it was necessary for there to be some kind of a consensus on the *raison d'être* of the Christian concern for development, which would be a guide-line for all the activities of the churches. The position paper on the "Debate about Development" asked how the churches could ensure that the positions they took by their actions were theologically tenable, though it was stated at the same time that it seemed to be mischievous to appeal to a theological understanding of development to justify any particular involvement. However, should there not be a vision of the developed society, and should we not strive for a precise definition of such terms as "development", "justice", "humanisation" and "liberation"? The position paper stated that as soon as the whole spectrum of life was included in the "ends" of development, it became clear that development was not synonymous with becoming richer, either materially or socially. To that extent development would cease to be an activity pursued only by the poor countries. The rich countries were recognized to be as badly in need of development as the poor.

Dr. Hamilton of the Pearson Commission argued that efforts to raise income should not be deferred until we had defined and, presumably, achieved real development. He therefore warned the churches not to delay action pending a general "theory" of development.

Similarly, Dom Helder Camara appealed to the churches to carry out the fine convictions expressed in the reports from Uppsala and Beirut. "For the next few years", Bishop Camara stated, "we Christians do not require any more documents concerning the social sphere. The problem that we now have to tackle is that of putting our fine theories into practice".

Even though Dr. Hamilton sounded a note of warning to introduce non-economic elements into the development process, arguing that they offered a risk of dissolving the whole basis of joint action by rich and poor, it became obvious that the churches' involvement in development had to bring forth the Christian concern for the freedom and dignity of each and every human-being in God's creation.

This Christian vision of development would have to transcend the technical concept which aimed at economic growth, even at the expense of growing national and international injustices. While economic performance is an important factor in the development process of a nation. Professor Parmar made it clear that social justice was the over-arching goal of development within which the two other important goals, namely self-reliance and economic growth, should be integrated. Social justice incorporated equality and human dignity. It implied a more equitable distribution of resources and economic power, and new relationships between social groups so that development of one did not depend upon or lead to deprivation of the other.

Professor Parmar further pointed to the fact that "domestic imperialism" was the root cause of instability and upheaval in many developing countries. Many of these struggles, even though they took ethic, tribal, cultural and linguistic forms, constituted a part of the quest for equality and human dignity. At the moment, there was evidence that the "green revolution", designed as an instrument of social transformation, had become another weapon of social oppression. This was due to out-moded agrarian structures and to the fact that the new technology and strategy had been geared to the goals of production to the neglect of social imperatives.

Thus, it became clear that development could not take place without radical changes in economic and social relationships and diffusion of political power. The kind of stability which was defended by those who had a vested interest in the undisturbed continuance of present political, economic and social structures was change-resisting, hence development-denying. Christians, however, had made considerable efforts in order to defend this very stability. In fact, they had come to accept as "social order", structures which protected the privileges of a minority at the expense of the poverty of millions. Dom Helder Camara rightly pointed to the follies and cruelties which were committed on the pretext of preventing subversion and combatting communism. Communism had become the scape-goat of society which justified the maintenance of structures in which centuries of violence were entrenched.

142

The need for a profound transformation in the political, ideological and social systems of the world today also resounded in the final reports of the Consultation: it was stated that if such transformation did not take place, the very process of development tended to accentuate disparities and increase the power of the dominant group. There was need for the churches to become more aware of the growing disparities of the poor, dispossessed and powerless and the accumulation of wealth and power. They also had to become aware that the challenges of development affected people around the world, both in developing and developed countries. Such awareness would have to lead to a new understanding of development, based upon new criteria of the social and the human. It would make the developed nations conscious of the spheres of underdevelopment in their own societies. It was further stated that such a new concept of development would have to lead to specific actions: if it was true that all societies were "developing", then they (and their churches) had to refuse to become merely "donors" or "receivers". They would have to learn the real meaning of interdependence, i. e. how "developing" countries could become "donors" and vice versa. This concept of development would also have to be reflected in the methods of financial assistance: a new venture would have to begin with a systematic support from the entire ecumenical fellowship.

Work in development, should not consist of isolated projects, but of inter-related programmes. The criteria of such programmes should be self-determination as to the goals and structures, and a dynamic conception of social justice, which alone could promote a satisfactory rate of economic growth and ensure programmes towards self-reliance.

There was certainly no consensus on the question of how to create a society based on social justice. Frequent reference was made to the fact that measures of distributive justice aimed at bridging the existing gap between rich and poor at national and international levels, met with structures which prevented their implementation.

Thus, Professor Parmar pointed to the fact that it was precisely the existing social framework which was responsible for the "lack of political will", which was usually identified as the main obstacle to more egalitarian international economic policies. Does the change of the social framework necessitate a revolution? Professor Parmar argued that, as the process of development entailed change, instability, disorder and upheaval, development might well be defined as revolution. He made it clear, however, that the objective of revolution was to acquire power in order to establish institutions and policies that would lead to certain social goals. A purely anti-institutional view of revolution would be *laissez faire*-ist and reactionary. Tearing down served a specific function in the process of development: it would create space to build a new.

While Professor Parmar raised a strong voice for a radical approach to the problems of restructuring society, Minister Eppler believed that a peaceful change of structures was possible, even given the present distribution of power and wealth. He advocated that changes should be promoted in a pragmatic way without endangering the small degree of order, regulated communication among the states, economies and societies and humanity that was still left after the era of colonialism and world wars. Such a pragmatic approach would have to start off in a flexible, puralistic, perhaps even contradictory manner. It would have to appeal to the common sense in the ruling forces, while at the same time, encouraging and promoting reformist groups and remaining in contact with the revolutionary element.

The practical suggestions for ecumenical assistance for development projects naturally reflected the train of these theoretical considerations. The position paper on "Policy and Procedures for Church Support of Projects of Development" had asked which kind of programmes the churches should support. Was it true that the churches had a special vocation, for instance, to work amongst the most needy or amongst groups who, precisely as a result of development processes, became worse off either materially or in other ways?

Dr. Eppler and Dr. Gardiner voiced the special concern the churches should have for those who are usually by-passed by development. Dr. Eppler held that the churches must often go out to where man lived in misery and not stop once the area of maximum profitability was left behind. Dr. Gardiner pointed to the fact that it was generally argued that it was not possible both to help the poorest people and to promote development at the same time, because these people were the ones who were least responsive to new ideas and techniques. He suggested that the churches should consider a systematic assault on this basic contradiction in current development experience and thinking. Professor Parmar was concerned about practical ways in which the style of operation of ecumenically assisted projects could reflect social justice, promote self-reliance and serve the larger goals of development.

The final report took up the challenge of these suggestions and pointed at specific types of programmes which were considered appropriate for church action. Such programmes should promote social justice and self-reliance of the community. They should help to provide new creative patterns of life for groups and communities whose lives had been disrupted by the effects of economic growth, and they should help to build bridges between seperated groups in the interest of a more integrated society. The Group also recommended co-operation with intergovermental agencies, especially of the U.N. Development System. It was recognized that such co-operation was not usually a matter of simply supplying church funds, but rather an attempt to involve the participation of the local church in planning or in operation. Operational co-operation could try to encourage the local community to participate in a project and accept the changes that it might bring about. It could plan subsidiary projects of a social kind and follow up programmes spreading the benefit of a project to the population. There was also need for the churches to work independently in order to undertake pioneering tasks not yet taken up by governments in their development plans, and to take calculated risks in setting up projects to prove new techniques.

That the churches should make use of their unusual capacity to attract dedicated people, and their unique geographical spread as well as their vast stock of experience in the fields of education, medical care and social welfare services was a frequently recurring theme. Professor Parmar suggested that established Christian agencies serving in these fields should be considered for taking up responsibility for development projects. A linking-up with projects of this kind might enable existing institutions to recapture their pioneering heritage and might, indeed, render them agents of social change.

As the operational goals for projects and programmes must be expressed and adopted at the level of a single country, the requirement most basic to an effective involvement in development was the need of a permanent mission in the developing countries where substantial programmes were undertaken. Dr. Hamilton invited the churches to establish such central field missions. They should be ecumenical in character and divorced from proselytizing and other parochial activities. Properly designed, financed and staffed they could well become responsible for conceiving and preparing development projects, negotiating with hosts and collaborators, evaluating results and advising the constituent confessions with respect to both past and future. Dr. Eppler too stressed the need for regional development institutions.

The final report recommended that national or regional counterpart groups be set up, which should become responsible for national or regional planning and co-ordination as well as the determination of adequate priorities.

It was also recommended that the churches embark on a study programme similar to the programmes already carried out by several international organisations. Thus, Dr. Eppler suggested that the churches should set up an independent international study centre which could tackle the questions pertaining to change of social structures. The churches would be especially qualified to set up such an institution as they were not bound by governmental obligations and by the principle of non-interference into internal affairs in the strict sense of the word. Experts working at the international study centre could stand back and take a hard, objective and thorough look at the development policies of national governments and international organisations and judge them, above all, in the light of clear social standards. The need for such study programmes was also implicit in Dr. Hamilton's suggestion that the churches should try to promote the humanitarian case for development aid. It was also felt that it was necessary for the churches to undertake a critical review of whether their projects and programmes promoted fundamental social justice or whether they were only marginal palliatives which might actually prevent profound change. It was recommended that emphasis be put on research related to informed and self critical decision-making.

Professor Parmar called for research which would evolve techniques with greater indigenous orientation, which would utilize resources available in the country and unearth and create new resources. This would help to promote self-reliance in ideas and authentic social

146

thought based upon the ethos of a respective society and geared to its problems and potentialities.

Similarly, Professor André Philip called for a new approach to what is called in English "technical assistance". He held that the French term *"coopération technique"* already represented a step forward, and might help prepare the way for a change of present patterns of technical assistance. He proposed an international pool of technical experts upon which any country could draw whenever necessary, in order to carry out the projects it has chosen itself.

These suggestions were taken up by the group who tried to work out guide-lines for technical assistance to church sponsored development projects. The Group agreed that the primary task was to stimulate and promote technical creativity in the developing countries. It was realized that present patterns of technical co-operation hinged on the fallacious idea of transferring knowledge and techniques from the materially developed countries to less-developed countries, on the assumption that these ideas were of high quality and suited to the needs of the latter. These patterns fostered a passive and often alienating imitation of models prevailing in dominant countries, and frequently they reflected interests other than those of the local community. The purpose of technical assistance would, therefore, be to awaken the talents, self-respect, dignity and critical spirit of nationals, both technicians and others, and to ensure their participation in the construction or reconstruction of their societies.

It was generally recognized that the churches had a unique opportunity to educate and sensitize the public. Dr. Hamilton outlined the possible role of the churches in persuading governments to organise themselves under multilateral auspices to mount a new campaign for development cooperation, and Dom Helder Camara made specific suggestions for a joint action of the World Council of Churches and the Pontifical Commission Justice and Peace. Together these bodies could create a movement of public opinion on the European scale which would perhaps bring moral pressure to bear leading to a change in structure there as a prior condition to bringing about a change in structure of the underdeveloped countries. The World Council and the Pontifical Commission should also make a move towards co-operating with the main religions of the world in order to bring all the moral forces they possess to an achievement of justice.

The Working Group which was concerned with the possibilities of mobilizing funds also regarded education and information to be of prime importance. The main question was how to raise more funds in view of the fact that a certain *compassion fatigue* limited the amount of money that could be raised in the traditional type of campaign. It was stated that *compassion fatigue* could be avoided only through an intellectual understanding of the nature and purpose of development. It was, therefore, recommended that part of the funds raised should be used for education programmes, the mobilization of public opinion and the financing of political action, especially in the affluent countries.

It was obvious that there was need for a structure which was capable of responding adequately to the new demand for development. The position paper concerned with this question had drawn up several possibilities of how ecumenical assistance for development projects could be provided. It had stated that ecumenical assistance could be confined to indentifying and selecting projects sponsored by governmental and intergovernmental agencies and commending them for support by the churches. It was also possible to provide assistance to already existing national, international and ecumenical agencies and to perform certain co-ordinating functions for these agencies. Further, one might propose to establish either a centrally administered development fund or regional development funds which would enable the representatives from the regions concerned to have the major responsibilities for decision-making processes. Finally, the need for a comprehensive programme of ecumenical assistance might call for an equally comprehensive approach to the problems involved.

The Consultation recommended that a new structure be established which should become the central unit of the WCC, where all programmes and projects related to development should be coordinated in the light of the findings of the Consultation and of insights arising from experience in the field. The work of other relevant units in the WCC and the knowledge available from governmental, intergovernmental and academic sources should be utilized. The new unit should be open and flexible to co-operation with other organisations, Christian or non-Christian. It should take into account that the primary responsibility for development programmes and projects would have to rest at the local, regional or national levels.

It should provide a forum for reflection of the meaning of development and the churches role in it. Furthermore, it should embark on programmes of development education, information and action leading to social change. It should also serve as a catalyst for multilateral planning and action and as a matchmaker bringing together the partners in development. Maximum co-operation with the Roman Catholic Church should be envisaged.

To meet those requirements the Consultation recommended to the World Council of Churches to set up a Commission on the Churches' Participation in Development Programmes. This Commission should consist of 20 to 25 members, all of which should be experts in development disciplines or experienced in the churches' involvement therein. At least one half of the members should be from developing areas. The mandate of the Commission should include study, reflection, and analysis of the churches' role in development, promotion of development education and information, and policy co-ordination in the choice and execution of development programmes and projects. The Commission would also be responsible for the administration of the Ecumenical Development Fund, suggested by Working Group V (The Mobilization of Funds). The Commission would have to work together, in the closest possible way, with those WCC units which are concerned with devolopment, as well as with SODEPAX.

Appendix II

List of Participants

ANDRIAMANJATO, Pastor
Richard Mayor, Politician

1 rue du Général Léon André,
Tananarive,
Madagascar.

APPEL, Rev. Dr. André
General Secretary

Lutheran World Federation,
150 Route de Ferney,
1211 Geneva 20,
Switzerland.

BEAUMONT, Pastor Jacques
Staff IRFED

IRFED,
47 - 49 rue de la Glacière,
Paris 13,
France.

BEERMANN, Dr. Victor A. M.
Adviser UNICEF

UNICEF,
United Nations Headquarters,
New York,
N.Y. 10017,
U.S.A.

BIELER, Dr. André
Professor

Route de l'Etraz 50,
1260 Nyon,
Switzerland.

BILHEIMER, Dr. Robert S.
Church Executive

Department of International
Affairs,
National Council of Churches,
475 Riverside Drive,
New York, N.Y. 10027,
U.S.A.

BLANC, Rev. Jacques
Director, Christian Service

Christian Committee for Service
in Algeria,
60 rue Larbi Ben M'Hidi,
Algeria.

BOS, Mr. J. Church Executive	Interchurch Coordination Committee for Development Aid, 17 Corn. Houtmanstraat, Utrecht, Holland.
BUKASA, Rev. Samuel Church Executive	Conseil protestant du Congo, B.P. 3094, Kinshasa, République démocratique du Congo.
BUMA, Rev. Kentaro Church Executive	National Christian Council of Japan, Bible House, 5-1, Ginza, 4-Chome, Tokyo, Japan.
CAMARA, Dom Helder Archbishop	Av. Rui Barbosa, S/N Recife, P.E. Brazil.
CASTILLO-CARDENAS, Dr. Gonzalo, Pastor	Apartado Aereo 14-650, Bogota 1, DE, Colombia.
CHANDY, Dr. Jacob Medical Doctor	Christian Medical College, Vellore, South India. at present: World Council of Churches, Christian Medical Commission, 150 Route de Ferney, 1211 Geneva, Switzerland.
CHAVEZ CAMPOS, Bishop Enrique Church Executive	Iglesia Pentecostal de Chile, Casilla de Correo 2, Curico, Chile.

CHIKOMO, Rev. Herbert P. Church Executive	Christian Council of Rhodesia, P.O. Box 3566, Salisbury, Rhodesia.
CHU, Mr. Yo-Han Former Cabinet Minister	80-17 Sajik Dong, Seoul, South Korea.
CUTHBERT, Rev. Robert W. M. Church Executive	Christian Action for Development in the Eastern Caribbean, P.O. Box 616, Bridgetown, Barbados, W.I.
DESUEZA, Rev. Edmond, Priest	Apartado 471, San Pedro de Macoris, Dominican Republic.
DICKINSON, Dr. Richard Professor	Christian Theological Seminary, 1000 West 42 Street, Indianapolis, Indiana 46208, U.S.A.
DUDBRIDGE, Mr. Bryan J. Church Executive	Christian Aid, P.O. Box 1, London S.W. 1., England.
EDGAR, Mr. James E. YMCA Secretary	World Alliance of YMCAs 37 Quai Wilson, 1201 Geneva, Switzerland.
ELLIOTT, Rev. Dr. Charles M. Economist, Pastor	World Council of Churches, SODEPAX, 150 Route de Ferney, 1211 Geneva 20, Switzerland.

EPPLER, Dr. Erhard Minister for Economic Cooperation	Bundesminister für Wirtschaftliche Zusammenarbeit, 5300 Bonn/Rhld., Kaiserstraße 185-197, Germany.
ERRAHMANI, Mr. A. B. UNESCO Executive	Funds in Trust Programme, UNESCO, Place Fontenoy, Paris 7, France.
FALS-BORDA, Prof. Orlando UN Executive	United Nations Research Institute for Social Development, Palais des Nations, 1211 Geneva 10, Switzerland.
FLORIN, Dr. Hans W. Church Executive	Evangelische Arbeitsgemeinschaft für Weltmission, 2000 Hamburg 13, Mittelweg 143, Germany.
FONSECA-TORRES, Prof. Dr. Irapuan Church Executive	Evangelical Confederation of Brazil, Caixa Postal 2428, Sao Paulo, Brazil.
GARDINER, Dr. Robert UN Executive	Economic Commission for Africa, Africa Hall, Addis Ababa, Ethiopia.
GOMEZ, Lic Fidel R. Sociologist	Rochester 65-3, Col. Napoles, Mexico 18, D.F.
GRACIA, Prof. Mathieu Professor	Institut Panafricain pour le Développement, B.P. 4078, Douala, Cameroun.

GRAHAM, Miss Betty C.
Church Executive

136 Woburn Avenue,
Toronto,
Canada.

GRAVES, Mr. Harold
World Bank Executive

International Bank for
Reconstruction and Development,
1818 H Street, N.W.,
Washington, D.C. 20433,
U.S.A.

HABIBY, Mr. Sami A.
Church Executive

P.O. Box 1231,
Amman,
H.K. of Jordan.

HAHN, Pastor Hans-Otto
Church Executive

Diakonisches Werk,
Innere Mission und Hilfswerk,
der Evangelischen Kirche
in Deutschland,
7000 Stuttgart 1,
Alexanderstraße 23,
Germany.

HAMILTON, Dr. Edward
Vice-President, Brookings
Institution

Brookings Institution
1775 Massachusetts Avenue N.W.,
Washington, DC.,
U.S.A.

HOOGEVEST, Miss Ruud van
YWCA Executive

World YWCA
37 Quai Wilson,
1201 Geneva,
Switzerland.

HOOVER, Miss Theressa
Church Executive

The United Methodist Church,
Board of Missions,
Women's Division,
475 Riverside Drive,
Room 1509,
New York, N.Y. 10027,
U.S.A.

HOUTART, Prof. François Priest, Sociologist	Université Catholique de Louvain, 116 Vlamingenstraat, 3000 Louvain, Belgium.
HOYSNIEME, Mr. Yrjö Church Executive	Finnish National Committee of the Lutheran World Federation, Vuorikatu 22 A. Helsinki 10, Finland.
HUERTA, Mr. J. Viteri de la UNCTAD Executive	UNCTAD, Palais des Nations, 1211 Geneva 10, Switzerland.
HUTASOIT, Mr. Marnixius Civil Servant	DGI, Djl. Salemba Raya 10, Djakarta IV/3, Indonesia.
JONES, Dr. Tracey K. Jr. Church Executive	Board of Missions of the United Methodist Church, 475 Riverside Drive, New York, N.Y. 10027 U.S.A.
KASTLUND, Director Åke Church Executive	Lutheran World Federation, Swedish National Committee, FACK, 18120 Lidingo 1, Sweden.
KEBEDE, Mr. Ato Abebe Director, Haile Selassie I Foundation	Haile Selassie I Foundation, P.O. Box 704, Addis Ababa, Ethiopia.
KOEV, Prof. Totiou Professor	Académie de Théologie, Place Lenine 19, Sofia, Bulgaria.

LAHAM, Mr. Albert
Lawyer

P.O. Box 4361,
Beirut,
Lebanon.

LEFRINGHAUSEN, Dr. Klaus
Professor

Sozialwissenschaftliches Institut
der Evang. Kirchen in
Deutschland,
463 Bochum,
Neustraße 7,
Germany.

LENGYEL, Mrs. Nina
Agronomist

77 rue Liotard,
1203 Geneva,
Switzerland.

LIM, Dr. Chong-Yah
Professor

University of Singapore
add Malaysia
Department of Economics,
Singapore 10.

LINNENBRINK, Dr. Günter
Church Executive

Evangelische Kirche in
Deutschland,
EKD-Kirchenkanzlei,
3000 Hannover 21,
Herrenhäuserstraße 2 A,
BRD.

LONG, Dr. Ernest E.
Church Executive

United Church of Canada,
United Church House,
85 St. Clair Ave. East,
Toronto 7,
Ontario,
Canada.

MACCRACKEN, Mr. James
Church Executive

Church World Service,
475 Riverside Drive,
New York, N.Y. 10027,
U.S.A.

MALONZO, Mr. Cipriano Trade Union Leader	Division of Mindanao Federation of Labour, Mezzanine Floor, Mariposa Building, F. Tanedo Street, Tarlac, Philippines.
MARO, Mr. Nicholas J. Church Executive	Christian Council of Tanzania, P.O. Box 2537, Dar-Es-Salaam, Tanzania.
MARSH, Rev. Clinton M. Church Executive	Ecumenical Programme for Emergency Action in Africa, 616 North Highland Avenue, Pittsburgh, Pennsylvania, U.S.A.
MATHAI, Mr. Stephen Church Executive	Christian Agency for Social Action, Relief and Development, 16 Ring Road, Lajpat Nagar IV, New Delhi 24, India.
MULIA, Dra. Wanda Lawyer	Sutan Sjahrir 46, Djakarta, Indonesia.
MYLONAS, Mr. Denis Economist	WCC/FFHC Liaison Officer for the YWP, Freedom from Hunger Campaign, Food and Agriculture Organization of the United Nations, Via delle Terme di Caracalla, 00100 Rome, Italy.

NICOLAS, Pastor Albert Church Executive	Fédération protestante de France, 47 rue de Clichy, Paris 9, France.
PALFY, Prof. Dr. Miklos Church Executive	Ecumenical Council of Churches in Hungary, Szabadsat Ter 2 I, Budapest 1, Hungary.
PARMAR, Prof. Dr. Samuel L. Economist	Holland Hall, Allahabad University, Allahabad U.P., India.
PERKINS, Rev. Harvey L. Church Executive	24 Foxall Street, Elanora Heights, NSW 2101, Australia.
PHILIP, Prof. André, Professor	Development Centre, OECD, 91 Boulevard Exelmans, Paris XVI, France.
PRONK, Dr. Johannes P. Economist	Schoenerstraat 12, Krimpen Aan De Lek, Netherlands.
RAJ, Mr. Daniel Sunanda ILO Executive	General Project Management Section, ILO, 1211 Geneva 22, Switzerland.
RANIVOARIMANANA, Miss Honorine Nutritionist	FAO Regional Office, P.O. Box 1628, Accra, Ghana.

RICHARDOT, Mr. Jean UNDP Executive	United Nations Development Programme, 866 United Nations Plaza, New York, N.Y. 10017, U.S.A.
RIES, Rev. Eugene Church Executive	Lutheran World Federation, 150 Route de Ferney 1211 Geneva 20, Switzerland.
ROMBA, Mr. Elie Civil Servant	B.P. 428, Fort Lamy, Tchad.
SABRA, Dr. Jesus Economist	Av. Canning 1261, Buenos Aires, Republic of Argentina.
SCHAFFERT, Pfarrer Hans Church Executive	HEKS, Stampfenbachstraße 123, 8006 Zürich, Switzerland.
SCHÜTTE, Fr. Johannes Church Executive	Pontifical Commission Justice and Peace, Piazza San Calisto 16, Vatican City.
SHAMS, Mr. M. M. Lawyer	Lahore High Court, 9 Rabbani Road, Old Anarkli, Lahore, West Pakistan.
SHERMAN, Dr. Charles Dunbar Economist, Financial Consultant to the President of Liberia	P.O. Box 66, Monrovia, Liberia.
SMITH, Dr. John Coventry Church Executive, President, World Council of Churches	UPUSA, Room 916, 475 Riverside Drive, New York, N.Y. 10027, U.S.A.

SØLLING, Mrs. Bodil
Church Executive

Church of Denmark
Inter-Church Aid and World
Service,
Kobmagergade 26,
1150 Kobenhavn, K,
Denmark.

SOVIK, Rev. Dr. Arne
Church Executive

Board of World Missions,
Lutheran Church in America,
231 Madison Avenue,
New York, N.Y. 10016,
U.S.A.

TAYLOR, Rev. Canon John V.
Church Executive

Church Missionary Society,
157 Waterloo Road,
London S.E. 1.
England.

THAN, U Kyaw
Church Executive

East Asia Christian Conference,
14/2 Pramuan Road,
Bangkok,
Thailand.

THIMME, Präses D. Hans
Church Executive

Altstädter Kirchplatz 5,
48 Bielefeld,
Germany.

TOLEN, Dr. Aaron
WSCF Africa Secretary

B.P. 790,
Yaoundé,
Cameroun

TROITSKY, Mr. German F.
Church Executive

Saint Synode de l'Eglise
orthodoxe russe,
Département des Affaires
ecclésiastiques extérieures,
18/2 rue Ryleev,
Moscou 34.

TSAOUSSIS, Mr. D. G.
Lawyer, Sociologist

20-22 Tzortz Street,
Athens 147,
Greece.

VANISTENDAEL, Mr. August Former Trade Union Leader	CIDSE, 59/61 avenue Adolphe Lacomblé, Brussels 4, Belgium.
VELASQUEZ VALLE, Rev. Roger Church Executive	Primera Iglesia Bautista de San Salvador, Avenida Cuscatlan 528, Apartado 1641, San Salvador, El Salvador.
VINAY, Pastor Tulio Social Worker	Servizio Cristiano, Via Faraci 79, Riesi, Sicily, Italy.
de VRIES, Prof. Egbert Sociologist	Graduate School of Public and International Affairs, University of Pittsburgh, Pittsburgh, Penna. 15213, U.S.A.
WEITZ, Mr. Charles H. FAO Executive	Freedom From Hunger Campaign, Food and Agriculture Organization of the United Nations, Via delle Terme di Caracalla, 00100 Rome, Italy.

Executive Staff
Would Council of Churches, 150 Route de Ferney, 1211 Geneva 20, Switzerland

ABRECHT, Rev. Paul R.   Church and Society

BARKAT, Dr. Anwar Masih   Division of Ecumenical Action

BAROT, Dr. Madeleine   Division of Inter-Church Aid, Refugee and World Service

BLAKE, Rev. Dr. Eugene C.   General Secretary

BOLIOLI, Rev. Oscar   Division of Ecumenical Action

BRASH, Rev. Alan A.   Co-opted Staff

BUHLER, Mrs. Ursula   Department of Communication

CARR, Rev. Canon Burgess   Division of Inter-Church Aid, Refugee and World Service

FAGLEY, Rev. Dr. Richard M.   Commission of the Churches on International Affairs

FISCHER, Mr. Jean   Division of Inter-Church Aid, Refugee and World Service

FITZSIMONS, Mr. Bevin   Ecumenical Church Loan Fund

FORKER, Rev. Wilbert   Department of Communication

GOERTZ, Rev. Marc   Department of Communication

GRUBER, Miss Pamela H.   Division of Ecumenical Action

HEUVEL, Rev. Dr. Albert H. van den   Department of Communication

ITTY, Mr. C. I.   Coordinating Committee on Development

JACKSON, Mr. Graeme C.   Division of Inter-Church-Aid, Refugee and World Service

† KITAGAWA, Rev. Dr. Daisuke	Division of World Mission and Evangelism
MCGILVRAY, Mr. James C.	Division of World Mission and Evangelism
† MURRAY, Mr. Geoffrey	Division of Inter-Church Aid, Refugee and World Service
NIILUS, Mr. Leopoldo	Commission of the Churches on International Affairs
NORTHAM, Mr. Frank	Department of Finance and Administration
SMITH, Miss Frances	Department of Communication
STRONG, Rev. Robbins	Division of World Mission and Evangelism
TAYLOR, Mr. John P.	Department of Communication
TRAITLER, Dr. Reinhild	Documentation Centre
de VRIES, Rev. C. Michael	Department of Communication
WEIL, Mr. Luiz Carlos	Advisory Committee on Technical Services
WHITTLE, Mr. Stephen	Co-opted Staff

Appendix III
Abbreviations

ACTS	Advisory Committee on Technical Services
CCIA	Churches' Commission on International Affairs
CIDSE	International Cooperation for Socio-Economic Development
DEA	Division of Ecumenical Action
DICARWS	Division of Inter-Church Aid, Refugee and World Service
DWME	Division of World Mission and Evangelism
ECLOF	Ecumenical Church Loan Fund
ECOSOC	Economic and Social Council
FAO	Food and Agriculture Organisation
GDP	Gross Domestic Product
GNP	Gross National Product
ILO	International Labour Organisation
IRFED	Institut International de Recherche et de Formation en Vue du Développement Harmonisé
NCC	National Council of Churches
OXFAM	Oxford Committee for Famine Relief
SODEPAX	Joint Committee on Society, Development and Peace
UN	United Nations
UNCTAD	United Nations Conference on Trade and Development
UNDP	United Nations Development Programme
UNESCO	United Nations Educational, Scientific and Cultural Organisation
UNICEF	United Nations Children's Fund
UNIDO	United Nations Industrial Development Organisation
WCC	World Council of Churches

Development
in the perspective of
World Council of Churches Publications

WORLD DEVELOPMENT
Challenge to the Churches

65 pp., 1968   SFr/DM 3.50   7s. $ 1.00

The conference for World Development in Beirut, Lebanon, 21 to 27 April, 1968, was sponsored jointly by the Roman Catholic Church and the WCC. The report considers the doctrinal, moral and ethical aspects of the development issue as seen by the churches.

THE DEVELOPMENT CHALLENGE
The Report of the Montreal Conference

37 pp., 1970   SFr/DM 1.50   3s. $ —.50

Report of a development conference held in Montreal in May 1969 sponsored by SODEPAX. This consultation was based on the results of the Beirut meeting in 1968 and reexamines some of the main issues discussed there.

LINE AND PLUMMET
The Churches and Socio-Economic Development in the Third World
by Richard Dickinson

112 pp., 1968   SFr/DM 6.80   13s.6d. $ 1.80

This brochure is a blueprint for a strategy on development of the churches. Three major factors are considered as being important: clear recognition of the motives, the situation and the available in-struments and institutions.

UPPSALA SPEAKS

Section Reports of the Fourth Assembly of the WCC
edited by Norman Goodall

97 pp., 1968   SFr/DM 4.80   9s.6d. $ 1.50

The Section Reports of the Fourth Assembly of the WCC in Uppsala
deal with the issue of development in Sections III and IV.

WORLD CONFERENCE ON CHURCH AND SOCIETY

edited by M. M. Thomas and Paul Abrecht

232 pp., 1967   SFr/DM 5,80   10s.6d. $ 1.50

The official report of the Conference in Geneva 1966 questions the
traditional attitude of the Church and calls for a new Christian social
ethic in the light of present technical, economic and political development.

A WORLD BROKEN BY UNSHARED BREAD

by Darroll M. Bryant

80 pp., 1970   SFr/DM 4.50   9s. $ 1.20

The study appears in immediate connection with the Fifth Assembly
of the Lutheran World Federation, held in Evian, France, in July
1970, under the theme "SENT INTO THE WORLD". The booklet
is offered especially to young people facing "the challenge of a hungry
world".

DEVELOPMENT EDUCATION

46 pp., 1969   SFr/DM 3.50   fs. $ 1.00

Report of the Consultation organized in Geneva in May 1969 by the
Secretariat on Development Education of the World Council of
Churches.

WORLD COUNCIL OF CHURCHES PUBLICATIONS

150, route de Ferney, CH-1211 Geneva 20, Switzerland

1. Professor André Philip (centre) from OECD, one of the speakers at the consultation, in conversation with Dr. Elfan Rees (left) of CCIA and Dr. K. C. Joseph of DICARWS.

2. A radio interview with Dr. Erhard Eppler, Minister for Economic Cooperation in the Bonn Government.

3. Dr. Eugene Carson Blake, General Secretary of the WCC, greets Archbishop Helder Camara of Recifé.

4. Dr. Eppler replies to a question. Dr. Blake, Archbishop Camara and Mr. Charles Sherman, chairman of the Consultation, take note.

5. A Latin American participant, Dr. Gonzalo Castillo-Gardenas, makes a point to Working Group I.

6. Dr. Robert Gardiner of the UN Economic Commission for Africa, making his presentation.

7. The Consultation in plenary session.

8. Dr. Eugene Carson Blake, Mr. C. I. Itty, organising secretary of the Consultation, and Mr. Charles Sherman study a working paper.

9. Two of the main speakers at the Consultation, Professor Samuel Parmar (left) of Allahabad University, India, and Dr. Edward Hamilton, vice-president of the Brookings Institution, Washington.

10. Archbishop Camara under siege from the Press.